A MACHINE MADE THIS BOOK

ten sketches of computer science

How do we decide where to put ink on a page to draw letters and pictures? How can computers represent all the world's languages and writing systems? What exactly is a computer program, what and how does it calculate, and how can we build one? Can we compress information to make it easier to store and quicker to transmit? How do newspapers print photographs with grey tones using just black ink and white paper? How are paragraphs laid out automatically on a page and split across multiple pages?

In *A Machine Made this Book*, using examples from the publishing industry, John Whitington introduces the fascinating discipline of Computer Science to the uninitiated.

JOHN WHITINGTON founded a company which builds software for electronic document processing. He studied, and taught, Computer Science at Queens' College, Cambridge. He has written textbooks before, but this is his first attempt at something for the popular audience.

A MACHINE MADE THIS BOOK

ten sketches of computer science

John Whitington

COHERENT PRESS

C O H E R E N T   P R E S S

Cambridge

Published in the United Kingdom by Coherent Press, Cambridge

© Coherent Press 2016

First published March 2016

A catalogue record for this book is available from the British Library

ISBN 978-0-9576711-2-6 Paperback

by the same author

PDF Explained (O'Reilly, 2012)
OCaml from the Very Beginning (Coherent, 2013)
More OCaml: Algorithms, Methods & Diversions (Coherent, 2014)

Contents

Preface

It can be tremendously difficult for an outsider to understand why computer scientists are interested in Computer Science. It is easy to see the sense of wonder of the astrophysicist, or of the evolutionary biologist or zoologist. We don't know too much about the mathematician, but we are in awe anyway. But Computer Science? Well, we suppose it must have to do with computers, at least. "Computer science is no more about computers than astronomy is about telescopes", the great Dutch computer scientist Edsger Dijkstra (1930–2002), wrote. That is to say, the computer is our tool for exploring this subject and for building things in its world, but it is not the world itself.

This book makes no attempt at completeness whatever. It is, as the subtitle suggests, a set of little sketches of the use of computer science to address the problems of book production. By looking from different angles at interesting challenges and pretty solutions, we hope to gain some insight into the essence of the thing.

I hope that, by the end, you will have some understanding of why these things interest computer scientists and, perhaps, you will find that some of them interest you.

Chapter 1 starts from nothing. We have a plain white page on which to place marks in ink to make letters and pictures. How do we decide where to put the ink? How can we draw a convincing straight line? Using a microscope, we will look at the effect of putting these marks on real paper using different printing techniques. We see how the problem and its solutions change if we are drawing on the computer screen instead of printing on paper. Having drawn lines, we build filled shapes.

Chapter 2 shows how to draw letters from a realistic typeface – letters which are made from curves and not just straight lines. We will see how typeface designers create such beautiful shapes, and how we might draw them on the page. A little geometry is involved, but nothing which can't be done with a pen and paper and a ruler. We fill these shapes to draw letters on the page, and deal with some surprising complications.

Chapter 3 describes how computers and communication equipment deal with human language, rather than just the numbers which are their native tongue. We see how the world's languages may be encoded in a standard form, and how we can tell the computer to display our text in different ways.

Chapter 4 introduces some actual computer programming, in the context of a method for conducting a search through an existing text to find pertinent words, as we might when constructing an index. We write a real program to search for a word in a given text, and look at ways to measure and improve its performance. We see how these techniques are used by the search engines we use every day.

Chapter 5 explores how to get a bookful of information into the computer to begin with. After a historical interlude concerning typewriters and similar devices from the nineteenth and early twentieth centuries, we consider modern methods. Then we look at how the Asian languages can be typed, even those which have hundreds of thousands or millions of symbols.

Chapter 6 deals with compression – that is, making words and images take up less space, without losing essential detail. However fast and capacious computers have become, it is still necessary to keep things as small as possible. As a practical example, we consider the method of compression used when sending faxes.

Chapter 7 introduces more programming, of a slightly different kind. We begin by seeing how computer programs calculate simple sums, following the familiar schoolboy rules. We then build more complicated things involving the processing of lists of items. By then end of the chapter, we have written a substantive, real, program.

Chapter 8 addresses the problem of reproducing colour or grey tone images using just black ink on white paper. How can we do this convincingly and automatically? We look at historical solutions to this problem from medieval times onwards, and try out some different modern methods for ourselves, comparing the results.

Chapter 9 looks again at typefaces. We investigate the principal typeface used in this book, Palatino, and some of its intricacies. We begin to see how letters are laid out next to each other to form a line of words on the page.

Chapter 10 shows how to lay out a page by describing how lines of letters are combined into paragraphs to build up a block of text. We learn how to split words with hyphens at the end of lines without ugliness, and we look at how this sort of layout was done before computers.

Acknowledgments

The word list on 67 is from *The Reading Teacher's Book of Lists*, Fourth Edition (Fry, Kress & Fountoukidis), Prentice Hall, 2000. The literary quotations used as example texts in Chapters 3 and the problems in Chapter 6 are from John Le Carré's *Tinker, Tailor, Soldier, Spy*. The text in Chapter 6 is from Franz Kafka's *The Trial*. Likewise in Chapter 10 from his *Metamorphosis*. The hyphenation examples in Chapter 10 are from *Micro-typographic extensions to the TEX typesetting system*, the PhD Thesis of Hàn Thế Thành, Faculty of Informatics, Masaryk University, Brno, October 2000. The cover image shows a Paige Compositor, courtesy of the United States Patent Office. The drawing of French Curves on page 17 was modified from one created by Joshua Certain. The tables on pages 35–39 appear by kind permission of the Unicode Consortium. Unicode is a registered trademark of Unicode, Inc. in the United States and other countries. The facsimile patents on pages 54,55,56,57, and 59 were provided by the United States Patent and Trademark Office. The picture of a Univac keyboard on page 60 appears courtesy of the Retrocomputing Society of Rhode Island. The picture of an IBM Model M keyboard on page 60 was taken by Sal Cangeloso. The woodblock print on page 101 is *Der Formschneider* (The Blockcutter) from the *Panoplia omnium illiberalium mechanicarum* (Book of Trades); it was printed in 1568 and is in the British Museum. The picture on page 102 is a detail of the engraving *Der Kreuzbrunnen zu Marienbad* published by Franz Sartori in 1819. The engraving *Melencolia I* by Albrecht Dürer on page 103 is held at the Minneapolis Institute of Art. The image of a mezzotint plate on page 104 was taken by David Ladmore. The picture of the mezzotint print by Franz Kruger on page 105 is courtesy of the Image Permanence Institute. The Rembrandt etching *The Hundred Guilder Print* on page 106 is held at the Rijksmuseum in Amsterdam. The photograph of film grain on page 108 was provided by Keith Cooper. The electron microscope image of film grain on the same page is courtesy of the University of Rochester. The halftoned picture of the Steinway Hall on East 14th Street in Manhattan on page 109 is from *The Daily Graphic*, December 2nd, 1873. The examples of Zapfino alternate glyphs on page 127 are based on the instructions of Dario Taraborelli. The tables of Palatino Linotype on pages 131–133 were produced using the eponymous typeface from Monotype GmbH. The sketches of metal typesetting on pages 142–143 are from an unknown early 20th century book. The photograph on page 144 was taken by Tom Garnett at the Print Shop of the Cambridge Museum of Technology, Cambridge, UK. All other photographs and images were created by the author. Scrabble is a trademark of Hasbro, Inc.

A MACHINE MADE THIS BOOK

ten sketches of computer science

Chapter 1

Putting Marks on Paper

In this book, we shall need very little formal mathematics, but if we are considering the arrangement of letters and words and lines and pictures on the page, we shall need a way of discussing the idea of position – that is to say, *where* something is, rather than just *what* it is. Thankfully, our paper is flat and rectangular, so we can use the simple coordinates we learned in school. In other words, we just measure how far we are above the bottom left corner of the page, and how far to the right. We can write this as a pair of numbers; for example, the coordinate $(6, 2)$ is six lengths right, and two lengths up from the bottom-left of the page. It is convention to use x to denote the across part of the coordinate, and y to denote the up part. These are known as *Cartesian* coordinates, named for René Descartes (1596–1659) – the Latin form of his name is Renatus Cartesius, which is a little closer to "Cartesian". The idea was discovered independently, at about the same time, by Pierre de Fermat (1601–1665). Here is the coordinate $(6, 2)$ drawn on a little graph, with axes for x and y, and little marks on the axes to make it easier to judge position by eye:

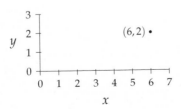

We can assign units if we like, such as centimetres or inches, to define what these "lengths" are. In publishing, we like to use a little unit called a *point* or *pt*, which is 1/72 of an inch. This is convenient because it allows us to talk mostly using whole numbers (it is easier to talk about 450pt than about 6.319 inches). We need such small units because the items on our page are quite small and must be carefully positioned (look at the writing on this page, and see how each tiny little shape representing a character is so carefully placed) Here is how an A4 page (which is about 595 pts wide and about 842 pts tall) might look:

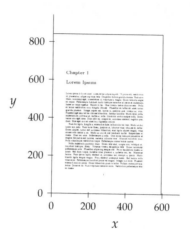

You can see that the chapter heading "Chapter 1" begins at about $(80, 630)$. Notice that the coordinates of the bottom left of the page (called the *origin*) are, of course, $(0, 0)$. The choice of the bottom left as our origin is somewhat arbitrary – one could make an argument that the top left point, with vertical positions measured downwards, is a more appropriate choice, at least in the West where we read top to bottom. Of course, one could also have the origin at the top right or bottom right, with horizontal positions measuring leftward.

We shall be using such coordinates to describe the position and shape of each part of each letter, each word, and each paragraph, as well as any drawings or photographs to be placed on the page. We will see how lines can be drawn between coordinates, and how to make the elegant curves which form the letters in a typeface.

Once we have determined what shapes we wish to put on each page, we must consider the final form of our document. You may be reading this as a physical paperback book, printed and bound by very expensive equipment. You may be reading it as an electronic document (such as a PDF file) on your computer, tablet, or smartphone. Or, you may be reading it on some sort of special-purpose eBook reader. Each of these scenarios has different characteristics. Every page of the printed book is made up of hundreds of millions of little dots, each of which may be white (no ink) or black (ink). We cannot typically see the dots with the naked eye. The number of dots is known as the *resolution* (from the word "resolve"). A low resolution image is one where it is easy for the eye to resolve (that is, distinguish) the individual dots. A high resolution image has dots so small and tightly packed that the naked eye cannot distinguish them.

A high resolution printer, such as the one printing the physical copy of this book, may have as many as 600 or 1200 dots per inch (dpi); that is to say, between $600 \times 600 = 360,000$ and $1200 \times 1200 = 1,440,000$ dots per square inch. The screen of a computer or tablet may only have 100 to 300 dpi, but it can display many shades of grey and colours. If the resolution is too low, we see blocky images. Here is part of a capital letter A in black and white at 60 dpi, 30 dpi, and 15 dpi:

We have used square dots here, such as may be used on a modern computer screen (we call them *pixels*, which is short for "picture elements"). For viewing a page on a typical tablet computer, we might have only $2048 \times 1536 = 5,193,728$ dots on the whole screen, but they may be colours or greys, as well as black or white. When printing a book like this, we have many more dots, but only black ink. Let us say, for example, that we have a US Letter page (8.5 inches by 11 inches) and we are printing at a resolution of 1200 dpi. We have $1200 \times 1200 = 1,440,000$ dots per square inch, so we have $1200 \times 1200 \times 8.5 \times 11$, or 134,640,000 dots on the page, each of which may be black or white.

Here are some photographs, taken under a microscope, of lettering as it appears in high quality printing, and on the much lower quality, cheaper newsprint used for the daily newspaper:

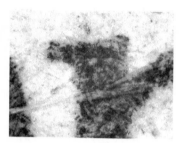

The upper row shows high-resolution printing of lettering on coated paper, such as might be used for a glossy pamphlet, under a microscope at 20x magnification, and the same at 400x magnification. The lower row is standard text of the London Times printed on newsprint at 20x magnification and the same at 400x magnification.

The home or office laser printer works by using a laser to prepare a roller in such a way that a powder will adhere only to areas where the laser has not been shone. The powder (called toner) is then transferred from the roller to paper, and bonded to it by heat. The particles of toner behave rather differently from ink:

On the left is a word printed in 1pt, 2pt, 4pt, 6pt, and 8pt text under a microscope, with magnification at 20x. On the right, the

2pt word with magnification at 400x (a typeface of a given size is roughly that number of points tall, say, for its capital letters.)

All these dots form a huge amount of information which is costly and difficult to manipulate. So, we will normally store our pages in a more structured way – some paragraphs, which are made of words, which are made of letters, which are drawn from some typeface, which is defined using lines and curves. The hundreds of millions of dots which will finally make up the page only exist temporarily as the image is printed, or placed onto the screen. (The exception, of course, is when we use photographs as part of our page – the colour of each dot is captured by the camera, and we must maintain it in that form.) Until recently the storage, communication, and manipulation of high resolution photographs was a significant problem. The storage, communication, and manipulation of high resolution video still is – imagine how many little coloured dots make up a still image, then multiply by 25 or 50 images per second for the 2 hours (7200 seconds) a feature film lasts.

We have talked only about single dots. However, we shall need lines, curves, and filled shapes to build our page. Suppose that we wish to draw a line. How can we work out which dots to paint black to represent the line? Horizontal and vertical lines seem easy – we just put ink on each dot in that row or column, for the whole length of the line. If we want a thicker line, we can ink multiple rows or columns either side of the original line. But there are many useful lines other than the horizontal and vertical ones. To begin, we shall need a way to define a line. We can just use two coordinates – those of the points at either end. For example, here is the line $(1,1)$—$(6,3)$:

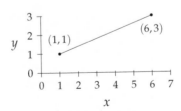

In mathematics, we would usually consider a line to be of infinite length, and so this is really a line *segment*, but we shall just call it a line. Notice that this line could equally be defined as $(6,3)$—$(1,1)$.

As a first strategy, let us try colouring in one dot in each column from column 1 to column 6, where the line is present. We will choose the dot whose centre is closest to the line in each case:

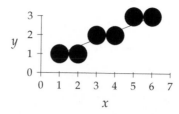

Admittedly, this does not look much like a line. But if we choose a higher resolution for a line of the same slope, and so draw more and smaller dots, we see a better approximation:

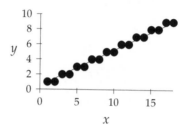

Now, you may wonder why we chose to draw one dot in each column instead of one dot in each row. For example, instead of putting one dot in each of the columns from column 1 to column 6, we might put one dot in each of the rows from row 1 to row 3, again choosing the one in that row nearest the actual line. For this shallow line, doing so would lead to a most unpleasant result:

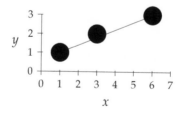

If the line is steeper than 45°, the converse is true (draw it on paper to see). So, we choose to put one black dot in each row instead of in each column in this case. Horizontal and vertical lines are simply special cases of this general method – for the vertical case we draw one dot in each row; for the horizontal case one dot in each column. For the line at exactly 45°, the two methods (row and column) produce the same result. Here is an illustration of the sorts of patterns of dots we see for lines of various slopes using this improved procedure:

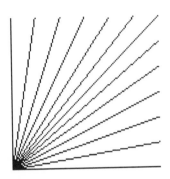

This image is 100 dots tall and wide. The results are not terribly good, for two reasons. First, at low resolutions, the individual dots are clearly visible. Moreover, the density of the lines varies. A horizontal or vertical line of length 100 will have 100 dots over its length, but the 45° line has 100 dots over a length of about 141 (the diagonal of a square with sides of length 100 is $\sqrt{2} \times 100$), and so its density of dots is lower, and it appears less dark.

When we are using a screen, rather than paper, to display our line, we can take advantage of the ability to use more than just black and white. And so, we can use varying shades of grey: dots which are right on the line are very dark grey, dots which are just close are lighter grey. Here is a line drawn in this manner, at three scales:

We can see that the line is smoother than would otherwise be the case. If you are reading this book on an electronic device, you may be able to see this effect on the text or images with a magnifying glass. Here is another example, with a more complex, filled shape, which might be used to represent an ampersand character:

On the left is an idealised high resolution shape. In the middle, just black and white at a lower resolution. On the right, prepared for display on a screen supporting grey as well as black and white, at the same lower resolution. This use of greys is known as *antialiasing*, since the jagged edges in low resolution lines are known as *aliasing*. This term originated in the field of signal processing and is used to describe problems stemming from low-resolution versions of high-resolution signals. Here is a photograph, taken under a microscope, of such an antialiased line on a modern computer screen:

The left image is magnified 20x; the right image 400x. The rectangular shapes you can see in the images are the separate Red, Green, and Blue sub-pixels, which a monitor uses to build up all the different colours and greys it may need (the monitor makes a picture by emitting light and Red, Green, and Blue are the primary colours of light.)

What might a reasonable minimum resolution be? To simplify, let's return to the scenario where we only have black and white dots – no antialiasing. The resolution required to make the page look smooth depends on the distance at which the typical viewer sees it. For a computer screen, this might be twenty inches. For a smartphone, eight inches. For a billboard, twenty or fifty feet (if you have never walked right up to a billboard and looked at the printing, do so – it is surprisingly coarse.) The limit of the human optical system's ability to distinguish the colour of adjacent dots, or their existence or absence, is the density of light sensitive cells on the retina. At a distance of 12 inches, a density of 600 dots per inch on the printed page may be required. For a billboard, we may only need 20 or 50 dots per inch. On a screen, antialiasing allows us to use a lower resolution than we might otherwise need.

We have seen how to draw lines between points, and so we can build shapes by chaining together multiple lines. For example, the lines $(1, 1)$—$(10, 1)$, $(10, 1)$—$(10, 10)$, $(10, 10)$—$(1, 10)$, and $(1, 10)$—$(1, 1)$ form a square (you can draw it on paper if you wish). We might define this more concisely as $(1, 1)$—$(10, 1)$—$(10, 10)$—$(1, 10)$—$(1, 1)$. However, if we wish to produce a filled shape (such as a letter in a word) we would have to make it up from lots of little horizontal lines or lots of little vertical ones, to make sure that every dot we wanted to be covered was covered. We should like to automate this process, so as to avoid manually specifying each part of the filled section. Consider the following child's picture of a house, made from several lines:

Notice that we have built three different sets of joined-up lines: one for the outline of the house, and two more, one for each window. Considering the bottom-left dot to be at $(0, 0)$, they are, in fact, these sets of lines:

for the house outline
$(1, 1)$—$(1, 10)$—$(9, 18)$—$(13, 14)$—$(13, 16)$—$(14, 16)$—$(14, 13)$—
$(17, 10)$—$(17, 1)$—$(11, 1)$—$(11, 5)$—$(7, 5)$—$(7, 1)$—$(1, 1)$

for the left window
$(3, 10)$—$(6, 10)$—$(6, 7)$—$(3, 7)$—$(3, 10)$

for the right window
$(12, 10)$—$(15, 10)$—$(15, 7)$—$(12, 7)$—$(12, 10)$

Now, we can proceed to design a method to fill the shape. For each row of the image, we begin on the left, and proceed rightward pixel-by-pixel. If we encounter a black dot, we remember, and enter filling mode. In filling mode, we fill every dot black, until we hit another dot which was already black – then we leave filling mode. Seeing another already-black dot puts us back into filling mode, and so on.

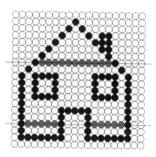

In the image above, two lines have been highlighted. In the first, we enter the shape once at the side of the roof, fill across, and then exit it at the right hand side of the roof. In the second, we fill a section, exit the shape when we hit the doorframe, enter it again at the other doorframe – filling again – and finally exit it. If we follow this procedure for the whole image, the house is filled as expected.

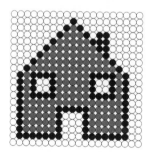 

The image on the left shows the new dots in grey; that on the right the final image. Notice that the windows and door did not cause a problem for our method.

We have now looked at the very basics of how to convert descriptions of shapes into patterns of dots suitable for a printer or screen. In the next chapter, we will consider the more complicated shapes needed to draw good typefaces, which consist not only of straight lines, but also curves.

Problems

Solutions on page 147.

Grids for you to photocopy or print out have been provided on page 173. Alternatively, use graph paper or draw your own grids.

1. Give sequences of coordinates which may be used to draw these sets of lines.

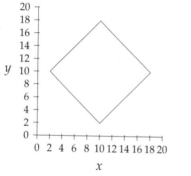 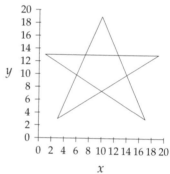

2. Draw these two sequences of coordinates on separate 20x20 grids, with lines between the points. What do they each show?

   (5,19)—(15,19)—(15,16)—(8,16)—(8,12)—(15,12)—(15,9)—
   (8,9)—(8,5)—(15,5)—(15,2)—(5,2)—(5,19)

   (0,5)—(10,10)—(5,0)—(10,3)—(15,0)—(10,10)—(20,5)—
   (17,10)—(20,15)—(10,10)—(15,20)—(10, 17)—(5, 20)—
   (10,10)—(0,15)—(3,10)—(0,5)

3. Given the following lines on 20x20 grids, select pixels to approximate them.

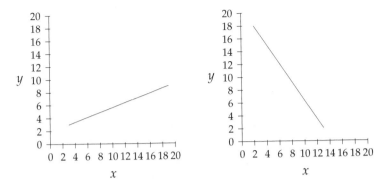

4. On 20x20 grids, choose pixels to fill in to approximate the following characters. Keep them in proportion to one another.

Chapter 2

Letter Forms

We have learnt how to build shapes from straight lines and how to draw those lines onto a screen built from pixels or onto paper using ink. If we only ever drew our shapes at one size, we could just use enough tiny little straight lines to build up any shape, including curved ones. However, we might like to draw our shapes at different sizes, or display them on devices with different resolutions. (There may be 1200 dots per inch on a commercial printer, for example, but only 200 dots per inch on a computer screen.) We don't really want to store a hundred little lines and their coordinates to describe a circle – we should just like to say "a circle of radius 20pt at coordinates (200, 300)", for example.

Consider the shapes which make up a letter of a typeface – *Palatino*, for example, which is used in this book. A typeface is a collection of little shapes, one for each letter, which are arranged on the page in lines. We must be able scale them to different sizes (large, for example, for chapter headings, or smaller for footnotes). They most often contain curves as well as straight lines. Consider the letter C, which has curved parts. The following diagram shows the effect of increasing the size of a letter C designed using only lines:

The straight lines survive scaling intact, but the curves are spoiled. Almost as simple as drawing lines (at least on paper) is drawing circles – we can do this with a pair of compasses. We could use these sections of circles (or arcs) to build our letter C instead:

This suffices only for simple letter forms. Imagine trying to draw complicated curves, such as the ampersand character, using just a pair of compasses:

Circular arcs don't help much here (not every curve is part of a circle). We would need dozens if not a hundred pieces of circles to accurately follow the shape of the letter.

Before computers, the solution was a set of *french curves*, which are shaped pieces of wood, rubber, or plastic whose contours are composed of curves of varying tightness. The curves are manipulated by moving and rotating them, until an appropriate contour is found for part of the desired shape. Sometimes this is done by starting with points through which the curve must pass, making it easier to line up the forms. A complex curve will be made up by using several different parts of the french curves, making sure that the joins between the chosen sections are smooth. Here is a typical set of french curves:

The curve sections used and points passed through can be recorded, so that the shape may be reproduced. Such curves are no longer used by draughtsmen, who use computers instead, but they are still used by, for example, dressmakers. A larger, less tightly curved set of shapes were formerly used for the design of boat hulls. They are known as ship curves.

How might we apply these techniques to computerised drawing? Two Frenchmen in the car industry, Pierre Bézier (1910–1999) at Renault and Paul de Casteljau (1930–) at Citroën, are responsible for the development of a kind of curve which is easy and predictable for the designer to work with, can be used to describe many useful sorts of shapes, and is amenable to manipulation and display by computer. They are known as Bézier curves.

We have seen that a straight line may be defined simply by its two end-points, for example (1, 3)—(6, 5). A Bézier curve is defined by four points: its two end-points, and two other points called *control points*, one for each end-point. These control points, which may be positioned anywhere, are used to pull the curve away from the straight line between the end-points. The further away the control points, the more the curve deviates from the straight line between its end-points. The following drawing exhibits several Bézier curves. (We have shown the control points linked to their respective end-points with dotted lines.)

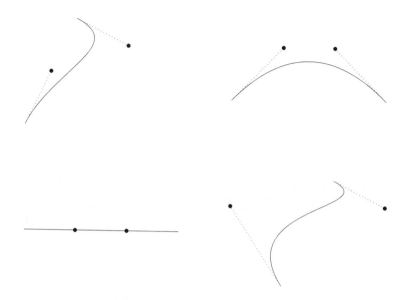

Note that a Bézier curve may bend one way or two, and that it may also be straight. The designer can move the control points interactively to build a wide range of curved lines. If you have access to an interactive graphics program on your computer, use it to play with the control points of a Bézier curve.

The curves we have made are still too simple to build a complicated shape, such as our ampersand. To make such shapes, we stitch together a number of such curves, making sure that an end-point of one curve coincides with an end-point of the next, forming a chain. A set of such chains for our ampersand is shown on the following page.

There are three chains of curves, which we call *paths*, in the ampersand: one for the main part and one each for the two "holes". There are 58 curves, of which 5 are straight lines. Note that several of these curves join very smoothly to one another. This is a matter of getting the control points for both curves in the right place: if the control-point associated with the end-point of one curve is arranged at 180° to the control point associated with the end-point of the next, the join will be smooth, with no change in slope at that point. Otherwise, there will be a definite corner. If the end-points of two adjacent curves in the sequence do not coincide at all, there will be a gap. (We call such curves discontinuous.) On the following page are examples of discontinuous, continuous, and smooth continuous Bézier curve pairs.

Bézier curve chains to draw an ampersand character

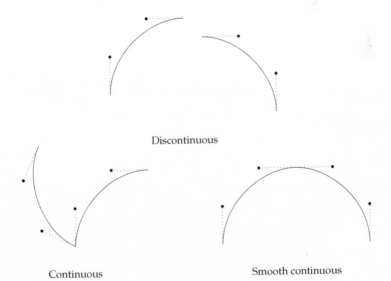

Discontinuous

Continuous   Smooth continuous

How can we draw a Bézier curve on the screen or print it on paper? It seems much more complicated than the straight lines we have already drawn. It turns out, though, that there is a simple way: we repeatedly split up the curve into smaller and smaller sections, until each one is almost as flat as a line. Then, we can draw each of those little lines using the method we developed in Chapter 1. How do we perform such a subdivision? We could pick equally-spaced points along the length of the curve. However, this would use too many lines where the curve is open, and too few when the curve is tight.

The following algorithm, devised by deCasteljau, is simple enough to do on paper, and produces a subdivision of the curve which is appropriate to the tightness of each part. Consider this curve with end-points A and D and control points B and C:

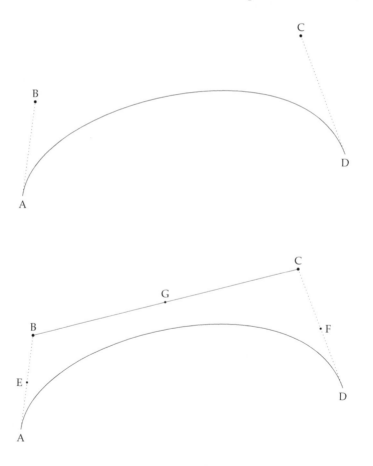

We have drawn the halfway points E and F on the lines between the end-points and control-points, and the point G halfway between the control points: Now, we draw lines between E and G, and between F and G, and find the halfway points H and I on those lines:

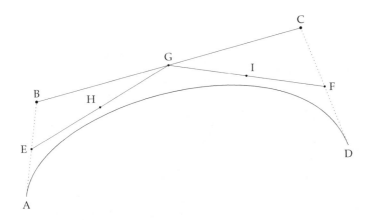

Halfway between those is the point J, which is the mid-point of the original curve, and the end-point of both new curves we are creating:

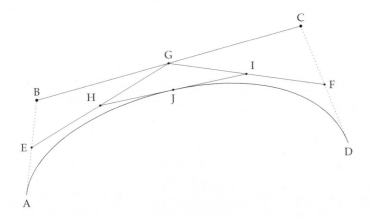

The two final curves can now be seen. They are, on the left, AEHJ and, on the right, JIFD:

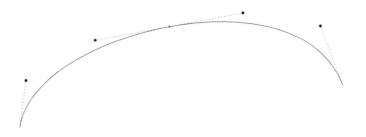

This procedure works for any Bézier curve. We can proceed to subdivide each of these smaller curves. Once we have subdivided enough times, each of the little curves should be flat enough to be roughly equivalent to a straight line between its end points. So we can just draw each as a straight line, using the procedure described in Chapter 1.

How do we decide when to stop the subdivision? If we stop after a fixed number of stages, the difference between the treatment of open and tight parts of the curve again becomes apparent. Instead, we calculate a crude measure of the "flatness" of a curve, and finish when that is less than a certain amount (say half the width of a pixel). A line is then an appropriate substitute for that curve. Here is a Bézier curve approximated by 1, 2, 4, 6, 7, 10, 13, 21, and 25 straight lines, as a result of repeated application of deCasteljau's procedure, stopping when each section is flat enough according to our test:

Here is one such approximate measure of flatness, which is relatively easy to calculate: the "height" of the curve. If the length $A + B$ in the diagram below is less than a given small number, we can approximate the curve with a line. This length will always be greater than the maximum deviation of the curve from the straight line joining its end-points.

We rejected the use of circular arcs due to their inflexibility, replacing them with Bézier curves, but there is an irony: no combination of Bézier curves can exactly represent a circle, or circular arc. However, we can get close enough. For a full circle, four Bézier curves will get us there. The following diagram shows circles built from two and four Bézier curves. Can you see the difference between the two "circles"?

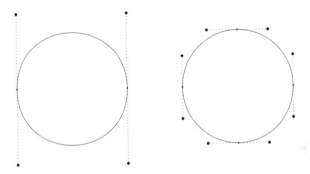

There is a further complication: how do we draw a letter which has a hole in it; for example, the letter O? We simply use two discontinuous paths – one for the outer circle and one for the inner:

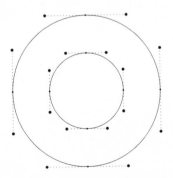

We have already looked, in the previous chapter, at a simple way to fill closed shapes like this. Let us formalise our method a little. When we fill such a shape, we fill any part where a line from that point to somewhere outside the letter crosses the shape an odd number of times. So, for our letter O, the inside path is not filled, as required. This is known as the *even-odd* filling rule.

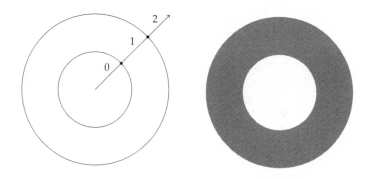

In the diagram above, we used a sloped line to count the crossings, whereas in the previous chapter we followed a horizontal row of pixels. It doesn't really matter; the result is the same. We don't paint points in the middle of the O because there are two crossings between there and outside the shape, and two is an even number. However, the even-odd method does not suffice when the path crosses itself. For example, consider the following self-crossing path – our even-odd method gives a peculiar and unwanted result:

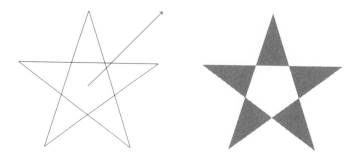

We can remedy this by changing the rule: now we shall look at the direction of the path at each point, counting one for each clockwise and minus one for each anti-clockwise crossing. We fill if the number is non-zero and the result is the one we want:

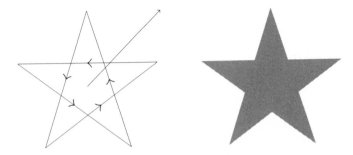

Our line crosses two anti-clockwise lines and is therefore non-zero (it has a count of $0 - 1 - 1$ which is -2). We can apply this rule to our O example too, but there is a problem: the inner hole is filled too:

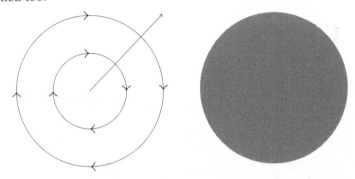

This can be fixed by reversing the direction of either of the two paths. We now have a method which works for both cases:

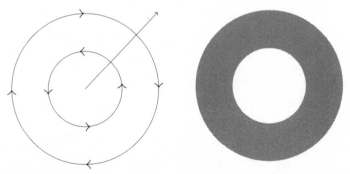

Now that we have some understanding of how to draw lines and curves onto paper or the screen, we will turn to the input, storage, and manipulation of text itself, before returning to the visual layout of the page later in the book.

Problems

Solutions on page 149.

1. Print out or trace the following Bézier curve, and divide it into two, using the procedure of deCasteljau. You will need a pencil and ruler.

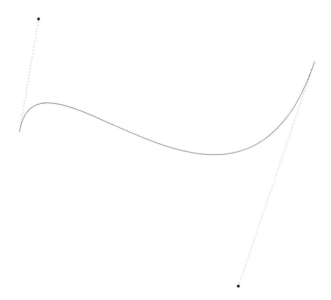

2. If you have access to a computer, find a drawing program with Bézier curves, and experiment to gain an intuitive understanding of how they are manipulated. At the time of writing, one such free program is Inkscape, suitable for most computers.

3. Fill in the following shapes using the even-odd filling rule and again using the non-zero filling rule. The direction of each line is indicated by the little arrows. The second and third pictures contain two separate, overlapping square paths.

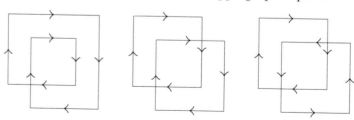

Chapter 3

Storing Words

Computers deal only in numbers. These numbers are processed in various ways, with no particular meaning assigned to them. However, we like to assign meaning, so we use a code to say which number means what. For example, we might set 0 = A, 1 = B, 2 = C etc. This code exists only in our heads and our computer programs – the computer itself still sees just numbers. From the very beginning, computers have been used to process textual data, to have textual input (from keyboards and similar devices), and to have textual output (to "line printers", which were a little like a conventional typewriter but connected to a computer, rather than a typist's keyboard).

Methods of encoding letters as numbers for communication have ancient origins. The Greek historian Polybius (c. 118 BC – c. 200 BC) relates a number of methods of communication in *The Histories*, including his own based on fire signals. The twenty-four letters of the Greek alphabet would be placed in a grid and reduced, in this way, to two numbers between one and five (the coordinates of the number in the grid). Here is such a grid for English (I and J must share a slot, since we have 26 letters):

	1	2	3	4	5
1	A	B	C	D	E
2	F	G	H	I/J	K
3	L	M	N	O	P
4	Q	R	S	T	U
5	V	W	X	Y	Z

Now we can signal a letter using just two numbers, each between 1 and 5. For example the word POLYBIUS, taking row first and column second, is 35–34–31–54–12–24–45–43. That is to say, P is at row 3, column 5, and so on. Now, to transmit a letter, we need only transmit two small numbers. Polybius's system used two banks of five torches. For P, we would set three torches to the up position on the left, and five on the right. The recipient would then set his torches the same way, to acknowledge receipt.

Computers, however, do not deal in fives – nor, indeed, in the tens and hundreds we do ordinary mathematics in. At the lowest level, we do not have ten things to choose from, or five, but just two: on and off, yes and no, the presence of electricity or its absence. However, computers can store and process millions or billions of such numbers. They are known as *bits*, and a bit is either off or on. We use the familiar digits 0 and 1 to represent them, 0 for off, 1 for on. If we are to represent letters using only one bit, we don't have many:

Bits	Number represented	Letter represented
0	0	A
1	1	B

Luckily, since we have billions of such bits, we can use more for each letter. When we add a bit, we double the number of bit combinations – and so, the number of representable letters. Now we have four:

Bits	Number	Letter
00	0	A
01	1	B
10	2	C
11	3	D

Add another bit, and we have eight:

Bits	Number	Letter
000	0	A
001	1	B
010	2	C
011	3	D
100	4	E
101	5	F
110	6	G
111	7	H

If we use eight bits, we have 256 slots available, from 0 to 255, which is enough, at least for all the usual characters and symbols in English.

Bits	Number
00000000	0
00000001	1
00000010	2
00000011	3
⋮	⋮
11111100	252
11111101	253
11111110	254
11111111	255

These 8-bit groups are very common, and so they have a special name. We call them *bytes*. In fact, we normally talk about something being 150 bytes in size, for example, rather than 1200 bits.

In the early days of computers, in the mid twentieth century, each organisation building a computer would design it mostly from scratch, with little regard for interoperability (that is, the ability for computers to talk to one another using the same codes). Since they might have been building the only computer in their country at the time, this was hardly a concern. Due to the size of the memory in these machines, and the characteristics of their design, the number of characters easily and efficiently represented was often small. For example, there may have been only 64 slots. There may not even be enough space for both uppercase and lowercase letters! There had been standardised codes before, of course, for telegraph communication, but they were largely disregarded. Let us take, as an example, the code used in the EDSAC (Electronic Delay Storage Automatic Calculator) computer at the University of Cambridge, which was built between 1946 and 1949. There were two sets of 32 characters, each represented by the numbers 0 to 31 – the "letter set" and the "figure set". Two of the characters were reserved for switching (or "shifting") between the two sets. This is rather like the shift key which we still use on keyboards today, to avoid having to have two sets of keys (one for lowercase and one for uppercase).

Letter set

0	P	8	I	16	null	24	lf
1	Q	9	O	17	F	25	L
2	W	10	J	18	cr	26	X
3	E	11	figs	19	D	27	G
4	R	12	S	20	space	28	A
5	T	13	Z	21	H	29	B
6	Y	14	K	22	N	30	C
7	U	15	lets	23	M	31	V

Figure set

0	0	8	8	16	null	24	lf
1	1	9	9	17	$	25	)
2	2	10	?	18	cr	26	/
3	3	11	figs	19	;	27	#
4	4	12	"	20	space	28	-
5	5	13	+	21	£	29	?
6	6	14	(	22	,	30	:
7	7	15	lets	23	.	31	=

In these tables, *figs* and *lets* are the letter and figure shifts. The *cr* and *lf* characters (as we shall see) are for moving the printing position around. The *null* character is often used for demarcation purposes; for example, to denote the end of a sequence of things. Notice that the letters are not in order and that there are no lowercase letters.

In order that computers may talk to each other, and so that the same program might run on different kinds of computers, standard codes have been developed. Here is the so-called ASCII (American Standard Code for Information Interchange) code, defined by an international consortium in the 1960s:

0	NUL	32	*space*	64	@	96	'
1	SOH	33	!	65	A	97	a
2	STX	34	"	66	B	98	b
3	ETX	35	#	67	C	99	c
4	EOT	36	$	68	D	100	d
5	ENQ	37	%	69	E	101	e
6	ACK	38	&	70	F	102	f
7	BEL	39	'	71	G	103	g
8	BS	40	(	72	H	104	h
9	TAB	41	)	73	I	105	i
10	LF	42	*	74	J	106	j
11	VT	43	+	75	K	107	k
12	FF	44	,	76	L	108	l
13	CR	45	-	77	M	109	m
14	SO	46	.	78	N	110	n
15	SI	47	/	79	O	111	o
16	DLE	48	0	80	P	112	p
17	DC1	49	1	81	Q	113	q
18	DC2	50	2	82	R	114	r
19	DC3	51	3	83	S	115	s
20	DC4	52	4	84	T	116	t
21	NAK	53	5	85	U	117	u
22	SYN	54	6	86	V	118	v
23	ETB	55	7	87	W	119	w
24	CAN	56	8	88	X	120	x
25	EM	57	9	89	Y	121	y
26	SUB	58	:	90	Z	122	z
27	ESC	59	;	91	[	123	{
28	FS	60	<	92	\	124	|
29	GS	61	=	93	]	125	}
30	RS	62	>	94	^	126	~
31	US	63	?	95	_	127	DEL

Some of these numbers represent real, printable characters, such as 65 for A. Others represent special codes, such as 13 for CR, which means Carriage Return and originally referred to the carriage of a typewriter-like device returning to the beginning of the line. Character 10 for LF, which means Line Feed, refers to a similar device shifting the paper up one line, so we may begin printing the next. The space character 32 moves one space across, without printing anything. Most of the other special codes are of historical interest only. We can work out the ASCII codes to represent a piece of text by looking at each character and finding its number in the table. Consider this quotation:

```
"It's the oldest question of all George.
 Who can spy on the spies?"
   -- John Le Carre, "Tinker, Tailor, Soldier, Spy"
```

Notice that we do not have the acute accent for the e in Mr Le Carré's name, and we have to use two dashes -- to make what would normally be the – long dash. There must be a Carriage Return, followed by a Line Feed at the end of each line, to move the printing position to the beginning of the next line. We obtain the following sequence of numbers:

"	34	l	108	s	115	T	84
I	73	space	32	p	112	i	105
t	116	G	71	i	105	n	110
'	39	e	101	e	101	n	110
s	115	o	111	s	115	k	107
space	32	r	114	?	63	e	101
t	116	g	103	"	34	r	114
h	104	e	101	cr	13	,	44
e	101	.	46	lf	10	space	32
space	32	cr	13	space	32	T	84
o	111	lf	10	space	32	a	97
l	108	space	32	space	32	i	105
d	100	w	119	-	45	l	108
e	101	h	104	-	45	o	111
s	115	o	111	space	32	r	114
t	116	space	32	J	74	,	44
space	32	c	99	o	111	space	32
q	113	a	97	h	104	S	83
u	117	n	110	n	110	o	111
e	101	space	32	space	32	l	108
s	115	s	115	L	76	d	100
t	116	p	112	e	101	i	105
i	105	y	121	space	32	e	101
o	111	space	32	C	67	r	114
n	110	o	111	a	97	,	44
space	32	n	110	r	114	space	32
o	111	space	32	r	114	S	83

f	102	t	116	e	101	p	112
space	32	h	104	,	44	y	121
a	97	e	101	space	32	"	34
l	108	space	32	"	34		

There are many more characters in the world than these, and therefore many proprietary and competing methods for extending this table. These include the addition of accented characters in the western languages, and the use of other methods altogether for the world's other character sets; for example, the Cyrillic characters of Russian, the Han characters of Chinese, and the many writing methods of languages from the Indian subcontinent. We shall examine some of these later in this chapter.

We have used the Carriage Return and Line Feed characters to change the way our text is laid out (sometimes called formatting). However, we have not seen how to change the typeface, *type shape*, **type thickness**, or the size of the text. We should like to be able to introduce such changes during the run of the text, as in this paragraph. What is needed is a way to "mark up" the text with annotations such as "make this word bold" or "change to type size 8pt here". Such methods are known as *mark-up languages*.

We could imagine a system where typing, for example, "This *word* must be bold" into the computer would produce "This **word** must be bold" on the printed page or electronic document. We could use a symbol for each other kind of change – for example, $ for italic – so we can write "$awful$" and get "*awful*". A problem arises, though. What if we wish to type a literal $ character? We must escape the clutches of the special formatting symbols temporarily. We do so using what is called an *escape character*. The most common is \ (the so-called backslash). We say that any character immediately following the escape character is to be rendered literally. So, we can write "And $especially$ for \$10" to produce "And *especially* for $10". How then do we type a backslash itself? Well, the backslash can escape itself just as well! We simply write \\. So, the literal text "The \\ character" produces "The \ character".

Let us look at how some common mark-up systems represent the following piece of formatted text:

Section Title

This is the *first* paragraph, which is **important**.

We might, for example, extend our system of special characters in the following fashion:

```
!Section Title!
This is the $first$ paragraph, which is *important*.
```

In the language used for web pages, the starting and ending signifiers (they are called "tags") are not symmetrical. A tag such as begins bold, the tag ends it. We also use <i> and </i> for italic, <h1> and </h1> for the heading, and <p> and </p> to explicitly mark paragraphs. (In the previous method, we had just used Carriage Returns and Line Feeds to mark them.) We may write:

```
<h1>Section Title</h1>
<p>This is the <i>first</i>, which is <b>important</b>.</p>
```

In the typesetting language used for writing this book, mark-up is introduced with the backslash escape character, followed by a descriptive name of the change being made, with the contents enclosed in curly brackets { and }:

```
\section{Section Title}
This is the \textit{first} paragraph, which is \textbf{important}.
```

Here, we have used \section{} for the section title, \textit{} for italic, and \textbf{} for bold. These differing mark-up systems are not just historical artefacts: they serve different purposes. The requirements may be wholly different for a document to be printed, to be put on the web, or to be viewed on an eBook reader.

We promised to talk about representing the world's many languages and writing systems. Since 1989, there has been an international industrial effort, under the Unicode initiative, to encode more than one hundred thousand characters, giving each a number, and defining how they may be combined in valid ways. There are more than a million total slots available for future use. It is important to say that the Unicode system is concerned only with assigning characters to numbers. It does not specify the shapes those characters take: that is a matter for typeface designers. The principle is one of separation of concerns: that each part of a computer system should do one job well and allow interaction with the other, similarly well-designed components. This is particularly difficult for the Unicode system, which must navigate innumerable cultural differences and a wide variety of possible uses.

The following five pages give some examples drawn from the huge Unicode standard.

	000	001	002	003	004	005	006	007
0	NUL 0000	DLE 0010	SP 0020	0 0030	@ 0040	P 0050	` 0060	p 0070
1	SOH 0001	DC1 0011	! 0021	1 0031	A 0041	Q 0051	a 0061	q 0071
2	STX 0002	DC2 0012	" 0022	2 0032	B 0042	R 0052	b 0062	r 0072
3	ETX 0003	DC3 0013	# 0023	3 0033	C 0043	S 0053	c 0063	s 0073
4	EOT 0004	DC4 0014	$ 0024	4 0034	D 0044	T 0054	d 0064	t 0074
5	ENQ 0005	NAK 0015	% 0025	5 0035	E 0045	U 0055	e 0065	u 0075
6	ACK 0006	SYN 0016	& 0026	6 0036	F 0046	V 0056	f 0066	v 0076
7	BEL 0007	ETB 0017	' 0027	7 0037	G 0047	W 0057	g 0067	w 0077
8	BS 0008	CAN 0018	(0028	8 0038	H 0048	X 0058	h 0068	x 0078
9	HT 0009	EM 0019	) 0029	9 0039	I 0049	Y 0059	i 0069	y 0079
A	LF 000A	SUB 001A	* 002A	: 003A	J 004A	Z 005A	j 006A	z 007A
B	VT 000B	ESC 001B	+ 002B	; 003B	K 004B	[005B	k 006B	{ 007B
C	FF 000C	FS 001C	, 002C	< 003C	L 004C	\ 005C	l 006C	| 007C
D	CR 000D	GS 001D	- 002D	= 003D	M 004D	] 005D	m 006D	} 007D
E	SO 000E	RS 001E	. 002E	> 003E	N 004E	^ 005E	n 006E	~ 007E
F	SI 000F	US 001F	/ 002F	? 003F	O 004F	_ 005F	o 006F	DEL 007F

UNICODE TABLE SHOWING THE ASCII CHARACTERS. They appear in the same places as in the ASCII standard – that is to say, if ASCII uses a particular number for the letter A, for example, so does the Unicode assignment. This is called *backward compatibility* and is hugely important in helping computer systems to continue to fit together over multi-decade timescales.

	008	009	00A	00B	00C	00D	00E	00F
0	XXX (0080)	DCS (0090)	NBSP (00A0)	° (00B0)	À (00C0)	Ð (00D0)	à (00E0)	ð (00F0)
1	XXX (0081)	PU1 (0091)	¡ (00A1)	± (00B1)	Á (00C1)	Ñ (00D1)	á (00E1)	ñ (00F1)
2	BPH (0082)	PU2 (0092)	¢ (00A2)	² (00B2)	Â (00C2)	Ò (00D2)	â (00E2)	ò (00F2)
3	NBH (0083)	STS (0093)	£ (00A3)	³ (00B3)	Ã (00C3)	Ó (00D3)	ã (00E3)	ó (00F3)
4	IND (0084)	CCH (0094)	¤ (00A4)	´ (00B4)	Ä (00C4)	Ô (00D4)	ä (00E4)	ô (00F4)
5	NEL (0085)	MW (0095)	¥ (00A5)	µ (00B5)	Å (00C5)	Õ (00D5)	å (00E5)	õ (00F5)
6	SSA (0086)	SPA (0096)	¦ (00A6)	¶ (00B6)	Æ (00C6)	Ö (00D6)	æ (00E6)	ö (00F6)
7	ESA (0087)	EPA (0097)	§ (00A7)	· (00B7)	Ç (00C7)	× (00D7)	ç (00E7)	÷ (00F7)
8	HTS (0088)	SOS (0098)	¨ (00A8)	¸ (00B8)	È (00C8)	Ø (00D8)	è (00E8)	ø (00F8)
9	HTJ (0089)	XXX (0099)	© (00A9)	¹ (00B9)	É (00C9)	Ù (00D9)	é (00E9)	ù (00F9)
A	VTS (008A)	SCI (009A)	ª (00AA)	º (00BA)	Ê (00CA)	Ú (00DA)	ê (00EA)	ú (00FA)
B	PLD (008B)	CSI (009B)	« (00AB)	» (00BB)	Ë (00CB)	Û (00DB)	ë (00EB)	û (00FB)
C	PLU (008C)	ST (009C)	¬ (00AC)	¼ (00BC)	Ì (00CC)	Ü (00DC)	ì (00EC)	ü (00FC)
D	RI (008D)	OSC (009D)	SHY (00AD)	½ (00BD)	Í (00CD)	Ý (00DD)	í (00ED)	ý (00FD)
E	SS2 (008E)	PM (009E)	® (00AE)	¾ (00BE)	Î (00CE)	Þ (00DE)	î (00EE)	þ (00FE)
F	SS3 (008F)	APC (009F)	¯ (00AF)	¿ (00BF)	Ï (00CF)	ß (00DF)	ï (00EF)	ÿ (00FF)

WESTERN ACCENTED CHARACTERS AND COMMON SYMBOLS. This is a subset of the common symbols and accented letters used in Western languages. Notice that some of the letters come with their accents attached, but some (for example, the cedilla in column 00B row 8) are made to be attached to several letters. Again, this is for historical reasons: for many years, it was not clear which was the best approach, and now the two must sit alongside one another. Such complexity is the disadvantage of backward compatibility.

	0E0	0E1	0E2	0E3	0E4	0E5	0E6	0E7
0		ฐ 0E10	ภ 0E20	ะ 0E30	เ 0E40	๐ 0E50		
1	ก 0E01	ฑ 0E11	ม 0E21	◌ั 0E31	แ 0E41	๑ 0E51		
2	ข 0E02	ฒ 0E12	ย 0E22	า 0E32	โ 0E42	๒ 0E52		
3	ฃ 0E03	ณ 0E13	ร 0E23	◌ำ 0E33	ใ 0E43	๓ 0E53		
4	ค 0E04	ด 0E14	ฤ 0E24	◌ิ 0E34	ไ 0E44	๔ 0E54		
5	ฅ 0E05	ต 0E15	ล 0E25	◌ี 0E35	ๅ 0E45	๕ 0E55		
6	ฆ 0E06	ถ 0E16	ฦ 0E26	◌ึ 0E36	ๆ 0E46	๖ 0E56		
7	ง 0E07	ท 0E17	ว 0E27	◌ื 0E37	◌็ 0E47	๗ 0E57		
8	จ 0E08	ธ 0E18	ศ 0E28	◌ุ 0E38	◌่ 0E48	๘ 0E58		
9	ฉ 0E09	น 0E19	ษ 0E29	◌ู 0E39	◌้ 0E49	๙ 0E59		
A	ช 0E0A	บ 0E1A	ส 0E2A	◌ฺ 0E3A	◌๊ 0E4A	๚ 0E5A		
B	ซ 0E0B	ป 0E1B	ห 0E2B		◌๋ 0E4B	๛ 0E5B		
C	ฌ 0E0C	ผ 0E1C	ฬ 0E2C		◌์ 0E4C			
D	ญ 0E0D	ฝ 0E1D	อ 0E2D		◌ํ 0E4D			
E	ฎ 0E0E	พ 0E1E	ฮ 0E2E		◌๎ 0E4E			
F	ฏ 0E0F	ฟ 0E1F	ฯ 0E2F	฿ 0E3F	๏ 0E4F			

THE THAI ALPHABET. Consonants are written left-to-right, with vowels arranged around them. The vowels are the characters in the table with little dotted circles. The dotted circle is not visible – it indicates the relative position of the consonant and vowel when the two are combined. The ฿ character is the only one with western origins – it is the currency symbol for the Thai Baht. This table is directly included into the Unicode standard from the existing Thai Industrial Standard TIS 620, simply with the numbers shifted. The Unicode system tries to do this whenever possible, for some level of backward compatibility.

	280	281	282	283	284	285	286	287	288	289	28A	28B	28C	28D	28E	28F
0	2800	2810	2820	2830	2840	2850	2860	2870	2880	2890	28A0	28B0	28C0	28D0	28E0	28F0
1	2801	2811	2821	2831	2841	2851	2861	2871	2881	2891	28A1	28B1	28C1	28D1	28E1	28F1
2	2802	2812	2822	2832	2842	2852	2862	2872	2882	2892	28A2	28B2	28C2	28D2	28E2	28F2
3	2803	2813	2823	2833	2843	2853	2863	2873	2883	2893	28A3	28B3	28C3	28D3	28E3	28F3
4	2804	2814	2824	2834	2844	2854	2864	2874	2884	2894	28A4	28B4	28C4	28D4	28E4	28F4
5	2805	2815	2825	2835	2845	2855	2865	2875	2885	2895	28A5	28B5	28C5	28D5	28E5	28F5
6	2806	2816	2826	2836	2846	2856	2866	2876	2886	2896	28A6	28B6	28C6	28D6	28E6	28F6
7	2807	2817	2827	2837	2847	2857	2867	2877	2887	2897	28A7	28B7	28C7	28D7	28E7	28F7
8	2808	2818	2828	2838	2848	2858	2868	2878	2888	2898	28A8	28B8	28C8	28D8	28E8	28F8
9	2809	2819	2829	2839	2849	2859	2869	2879	2889	2899	28A9	28B9	28C9	28D9	28E9	28F9
A	280A	281A	282A	283A	284A	285A	286A	287A	288A	289A	28AA	28BA	28CA	28DA	28EA	28FA
B	280B	281B	282B	283B	284B	285B	286B	287B	288B	289B	28AB	28BB	28CB	28DB	28EB	28FB
C	280C	281C	282C	283C	284C	285C	286C	287C	288C	289C	28AC	28BC	28CC	28DC	28EC	28FC
D	280D	281D	282D	283D	284D	285D	286D	287D	288D	289D	28AD	28BD	28CD	28DD	28ED	28FD
E	280E	281E	282E	283E	284E	285E	286E	287E	288E	289E	28AE	28BE	28CE	28DE	28EE	28FE
F	280F	281F	282F	283F	284F	285F	286F	287F	288F	289F	28AF	28BF	28CF	28DF	28EF	28FF

BRAILLE PATTERNS. The top section contains all those combinations using the top six dots only. (There were originally only six dots in Braille.) All the others then follow, for a total of 256. The patterns are not assigned particular letters, because these vary for each language: a pattern might represent the letter A in Western languages and something entirely different in Japanese or Vietnamese. Empty circles are used in most Braille typefaces so that, in patterns with only a few black dots, the empty circles can be felt with the finger to help distinguish between different characters. This is particularly useful when dealing with 8-dot patterns.

LINEAR A. An undeciphered writing system of ancient Greece, thought to have been in use 2500–1400 BC. It was added to the Unicode specification in 2014. We do not need to understand a writing system to reproduce it electronically! Most specimens were found on Crete, though they have been found as far apart as Bulgaria and Israel.

Problems

Solutions on page 151.

1. Using the method of Polybius, encode the phrase "MARY-HADALITTLELAMB". How many characters are in the message? How many numbers are needed to encode them? Can you think of a way to indicate the concept of "end of message" in Polybius's system? What about spaces?

2. Complete a table of bits, numbers, and letters for a system which uses five bits for each character. How many lines does the table have? Which characters did you deem important enough to include?

3. Decode the following message from ASCII: 84 114 101 97 115 111 110 105 115 118 101 114 121 109 117 99 104 97 109 97 116 116 101 114 111 102 104 97 98 105 116 44 83 109 105 108 101 121 100 101 99 105 100 101 100 46.

4. Encode the following message into ASCII: The more identities a man has, the more they express the person they conceal.

5. In a mark-up language in which \ is the escape character, and a pair of $s around a word means *italic* and a pair of *s around a word mean **bold**, give the marked-up text for the following literal pieces of text:

   a) The love of money is the root of **all** evil.

   b) The love of $$$ is the root of all evil.

   c) The love of *$$$* is the root of all evil.

   d) The love of **$$$** is the root of all evil.

Chapter 4

Looking and Finding

When writing a book, it is important to be able to wrangle efficiently a long piece of text. One important task is to search for a word, finding where it has been used: we may then jump to such a position in the text, see what is around the word, and modify or replace it. We need to do this on demand, without an explicitly prepared index. In fact, we have indexes at the back of books because searching through the book manually, from front to back, is slow and error prone for a human. Luckily, it is fast and accurate for a computer.

It might seem that it is easy to describe to a computer how to search for a word: just look for it! But we must prepare an explicit method, made of tiny little simple steps, for the computer to follow. Everything must be explained in perfect detail – no big assumptions, no hand-waving. Such a careful, explicit method is called an *algorithm*.

What are the basic operations from which we can build such an algorithm? Assume we have the text to be searched, and the word to search for, at hand. Each of them is made up of *characters* (A, x, ! etc). Assume also that we know how to compare two characters to see if they are alike or different. For example, A is the same as A but different from B. Let us pick a concrete example: we shall try to find the word "horses" in the text "houses and horses and hearses". Let us number each of the 29 characters in the text and the 6 characters in the word:

```
              1         2
T 012345678901234567890123456789012345678
  houses and horses and hearses

W 012345
  horses
```

We have called the text T and the word W. Notice that we number upwards from zero, not one. Let us begin by describing a simple searching method in the large, and then refine it into smaller steps. We shall be answering the question "Does the word appear in the text and, if so, where?", and the answer will be a series of zero, one, or more numbers giving the matching positions. Let us compare positions 0 to 5 in W with positions 0 to 5 in T. Plainly, they do not all match, though some of them do. Position 2 differs ("r" in the word W but "u" in the text T), and this is enough to declare failure. Now, we shall shift the whole word W onward one position and try again:

```
              1         2
T 012345678901234567890123456789012345678
  houses and horses and hearses

W  012345
   horses
```

Here, we fail on every character in our comparison. And we keep failing again and again, at each position we try, moving rightward one each time:

```
              1         2
T 012345678901234567890123456789012345678
  houses and horses and hearses

W            012345
             horses
```

Finally, though, we find the match (every character is the same), and we may declare that the word W was found at position 11 in the text T:

```
              1         2
T 012345678901234567890123456789012345678
  houses and horses and hearses

W            012345
             horses
```

If we reach a situation where the word overruns the end of the text, we stop immediately – no further match can now be found:

```
         1         2
T 012345678901234567890012345678
  houses and horses and hearses

W                      012345
                       horses
```

Let us try to write our algorithm out as a computer program. A program is a set of instructions written in a language which is understandable and unambiguous, both to the computer and to the human being writing it. First, we shall assume that the part of the program for comparing the word with the text at a given position already exists: we will write it later. For now, we shall concentrate on the part which decides where to start, where to stop, moves the word along the text position-by-position, and prints out any positions which match. For reasons of conciseness, we won't use a real programming language but a so-called *psuedocode* – that is to say, a language which closely resembles any number of programming languages, but contains only the complexities needed for describing the solution to our particular problem. First, we can define a new algorithm called search:

```
1  define search pt
```

We used the *keyword* **define** to say that we are defining a new algorithm. Keywords are things which are built into the programming language. We write them in bold. Then we gave it the name search. (This is arbitrary – we could have called it cauliflower if we had wanted.) We give the name of the thing this algorithm will work with, called a *parameter* – in our case pt, which will be a number keeping track of how far along the searching process we are (pt for *position in text*). We shall arrange for the value of pt to begin at 0 – the first character. Our algorithm doesn't do anything yet – if we asked the computer to run it, nothing would happen.

Now, what we should like to do is to make sure that we are not overrunning the end of the text – if we are, there can be no more matches. We are not overrunning if the position pt added to the length of the word W is less than or equal to the length of the text T, that is to say between these two positions:

```
          1         2
T 012345678901234567890012345678
  houses and horses and hearses

W 012345
  horses

W                    012345
                     horses
```

That is, when pt is between 0 and 23 inclusive. So, we write this condition into our program, using the **if**, **then**, and **length** keywords:

```
1  define search pt
2    if pt + length W <= length T then
3       . . .
```

The <= symbol means "less than or equal to". Note that the dots . . . at line 2 are not part of the program. They just show that we have not yet filled in what happens if our condition is true. (If our condition is not true, we do nothing, since we have finished searching.) We have indented (moved to the right) line 2 by two spaces as well. We use indentation to indicate structure in our program. Now to fill in the rest of the search procedure. We want to perform the comparison of the word with the text at the current position, and if it matches, we want to print out the position on the screen.

```
1  define search pt
2    if pt + length W <= length T then
3      if compare pt 0 then print pt
```

Here, we are using the yet-to-be-concocted compare algorithm to compare the text W with the text T at position pt. It has another parameter too, which it will use as a counter. We start it off at zero. We don't need to know how compare works yet: just what it does with what it is given. This convenient blindness is what allows us to construct programs piece by piece in a modular fashion, replacing individual parts without changing the rules which connect them. Now, whether or not we found a match, it is time to move on to the next position: we run search again, adding one to the position pt:

```
1  define search pt
2    if pt + length W <= length T then
3      if compare pt 0 then print pt
4      search (pt + 1)
```

Note that, due to the indentation, both lines 3 and 4 only happen if the **if** condition on line 2 is met. Now, see what happens when we execute our program on our example word "horses" and text "horses and houses and hearses":

```
W = "horses"
T = "houses and horses and hearses"
```

search 0	search 9	search 17
search 1	search 10	search 18
search 2	search 11	search 19
search 3	11	search 20
search 4	search 12	search 21
search 5	search 13	search 22
search 6	search 14	search 23
search 7	search 15	
search 8	search 16	

Here we have shown not only the matching position which our program prints, but a summary of the execution of our program, to help us to understand what is going on. A match is found – at position 11, as required – and the program stops after position 23. At least for this example, our program seems to work. Run through it on paper yourself to check. Now to fill in the gap: we pretended that compare already existed. In reality, we would have to write such an algorithm. We begin by defining it, just like for search:

```
1  define compare pt pw
```

The compare function will differ from the search one in an important way: the search function printed things to the screen – the compare algorithm will instead calculate one of two special values: either true or false. This will be passed back to the search function so it can decide what to do. The compare function has two parameters: the same one as search and one more, pw, which is the position in the word – we will first compare position pt in the text T with position pw in the word W, then pt + 1 with pw + 1 etc. Remember that when we wrote search, we started pw off at zero when using compare. As soon as we find a mismatch, we stop and return `false`. If we reach the end of the word without finding such a mismatch, we stop and return `true`, because the whole word must have matched. We dispense with the success condition first – if pw is equal to `length` pw, it means we have compared successfully positions 0 through to pw - 1, and so we can return `true`:

```
1  define compare pt pw
2    if pw = length W then return true
```

Now, we must test the character at position pt in T and the character at position pw in W to see if they are equal. We access the individual characters by writing, for example, `W[pw]` where W is the text and pw the position:

```
1  define compare pt pw
2    if pw = length W then return true
3    if T[pt] = W[pw] then compare (pt + 1) (pw + 1)
```

If the two characters were equal, we continue by running `compare` with both the text and word positions advanced by one. All that remains now is to return `false` if they were not equal:

```
1  define compare pt pw
2    if pw = length W then return true
3    if T[pt] = W[pw] then compare (pt + 1) (pw + 1)
4    return false
```

This line will only be reached if the condition at line 3 was `false`. Here is the whole program in one place:

```
1  define compare pt pw
2    if pw = length W then return true
3    if T[pt] = W[pw] then compare (pt + 1) (pw + 1)
4    return false
5
6  define search pt
7    if pt + length W <= length T then
8      if compare pt 0 then print pt
9      search (pt + 1)
```

Our made-up language is not so dissimilar to some real computer languages. Some of the words are different, but the essential features are there. Let us have a more detailed look at the execution of our search by giving a running commentary of the parameters given to search and compare:

```
W = "horses"
T = "houses and horses and hearses"
```

search 0	search 9	compare 15 0
compare 0 0	compare 9 0	search 16
compare 1 1	search 10	compare 16 0
search 1	compare 10 0	search 17
compare 1 0	search 11	compare 17 0
search 2	compare 11 0	search 18
compare 2 0	compare 11 1	compare 18 0
search 3	compare 11 2	search 19
compare 3 0	compare 11 3	compare 19 0
search 4	compare 11 4	search 20
compare 4 0	compare 11 5	compare 20 0
search 5	11	search 21
compare 5 0	search 12	compare 21 0
search 6	compare 12 0	search 22
compare 6 0	search 13	compare 22 0
search 7	compare 13 0	compare 22 1
compare 7 0	search 14	search 23
search 8	compare 14 0	compare 23 0
compare 8 0	search 15	

We can see that, most of the time, compare fails on the first letter in the word, and we need proceed no further. When a match is found, every letter must be checked, of course. At positions 0 and 22 we had to check more than the first letter to see that there was no match. You can run the whole thing through on paper, if you have the patience.

How much work did we have to do to find if there was a match? Let us consider comparing two letters as our basic unit of work – how many times did we have to do it? Consider Figure A over-leaf. We have made a total of 32 comparisons. (The number of comparisons is written at the right on each line.) We have made sure that our compare function fails as soon as possible, but have made no other efficiencies. We are lucky that "h" does not appear in English very often – if our search word began with "e" we would have to make many more second-letter comparisons. Let us call the length of the word l_W and the length of the text l_T, and find the minimum and maximum number of comparisons in general. In the best case, the word never matches on the first letter, so we

```
                   1         2
T 012345678901234567890123456789012345678
  houses and horses and hearses

W 012345
  horses  3
   horses  1
    horses  1
     horses  1
      horses  1
       horses  1
        horses  1
         horses  1
          horses  1
           horses  1
            horses  1
             horses  6
              horses  1
               horses  1
                horses  1
                 horses  1
                  horses  1
                   horses  1
                    horses  1
                     horses  1
                      horses  1
                       horses  1
                        horses  2
```

Figure A

always have one comparison each time. The total, then, is just $l_W - l_T + 1$ (We take away l_T because we stop when the word overruns the end of the text.) In our example, that is $29 - 6 + 1 = 24$ (for example, searching for zebras, since "z" will never match). In the worst case, we have to go all the way to the last character to see if a match occurs (for example, searching for "aaaaab" in "aaaaaaaaaaaaaaaaaaaaaaaaaaaaaa"). Then we need six comparisons for each position, which in general is $l_W \times (l_W + l_T + 1)$, or in our case $6 \times (29 - 6 + 1) = 6 \times 24 = 144$. Calculations such as these are vital in Computer Science. We must know how our algorithm performs as the size of the problem increases. This algorithm performs reasonably well: if the text size doubles, it takes twice as long, just as we might expect.

The field of searching algorithms is vast and complex, but we shall consider one of the simpler improvements: skipping forward more than one place when we know for some reason that a match cannot now happen. For example, let us consider the first position again:

```
           1         2
T 012345678901234567890123345678
  houses and horses and hearses

W 012345
  horses
```

The "h" matches, and then the "o", but the "r" in the word does not match the "u" in the text. Since there is no "u" anywhere in "horses", we can skip ahead to position 3 immediately:

```
           1         2
T 012345678901234567890123345678
  houses and horses and hearses

W 012345
  horses   3
       horses
```

Let us apply such skipping rules to our whole search, and see how many comparisons are now required. Look at the diagram overleaf. We skipped two times. The first time as described already – there is no "u" in the word "horses". The second time was when we found a match: since there is no "h" anywhere else in "horses" we may skip six places. We have reduced the number of comparisons from 32 to 23.

```
        1         2
T 012345678901234567890123456789012345678
  houses and horses and hearses

W 012345
  horses  3
     horses  1
      horses  1
       horses  1
        horses  1
         horses  1
          horses  1
           horses  1
            horses  1
             horses  6
                 horses  1
                  horses  1
                   horses  1
                    horses  1
                     horses  1
                      horses  1
```

We have produced a very simple searching method, and shown how it works. In reality, things are more complex. How do we deal with case ("Horses" vs. "horses"), different parts of speech ("horsed around with"), accents ("cafe" and "café"), ligatures ("haemoglobin" and "hæmoglobin") and so forth?

Of course, even with our existing search program, we can search for things other than words, such as "!!" to look for excessive punctuation, or "and and" to search for a common mistake. So let us stop calling the thing we search for a "word", and instead call it a *pattern*. The simplest examples of patterns are just what we have been using already: they find only a piece of the text which matches the pattern exactly. More advanced patterns consist of special characters to indicate a loosening of the requirements for one or more characters to match. For example, we can write realise|realize to search for either realise or realize. (The | symbol is on your computer keyboard, if you look carefully. In this context, we pronounce it "or" because it looks for the thing on its left, or the thing on its right, matching in either case.) In fact, we can simplify this pattern by using parentheses to limit the optional section, and write reali(s|z)e. This will still match realize and

realise. There are other special characters: we can use a full stop
. to match any character, so that the pattern .unce matches ounce
and dunce.

In addition to these patterns, we can run a search multiple times
and combine the results. For example, when using an internet
search engine, if we are interested in finding documents containing
"cats" or "dogs" we might enter the search "cats OR dogs". The
search engine knows that the word OR is special, and it runs two
searches, one for "cats" and one for "dogs" and returns documents
which contain an instance of either. In reality, search engines don't
look through the text of web pages at the moment that you click the
search button: they use pre-prepared indexes to make the search
many many times faster.

In the problems which follow, we extend this idea of patterns,
and ask you to run the searching algorithm through on paper to
determine whether they match the text.

Problems

Solutions on page 153.

1. Run the `search` procedure against the following patterns and this text:

   `The source of sorrow is the self itself`

   What happens each time?

   a) `cow`

   b) `row`

   c) `self`

   d) `the`

2. Consider the following kind of advanced pattern syntax and give example texts which match the following patterns. A question mark ? indicates that zero or one of the previous letter is to be matched; an asterisk * indicates zero or more; a plus sign + indicates one or more. Parentheses around two letters separated by a | allow either letter to occur. The letters ?, +, and * may follow such a closing parenthesis, with the effect of operating on whichever letter is chosen.

   a) `aa+`

   b) `ab?c`

   c) `ab*c`

   d) `a(b|c)*d`

3. Assuming we have a version of `search` which works for these advanced patterns, give the results of running it on the same text as in Problem 1.

   a) `r+ow`

   b) `(T|t)he`

   c) `(T|t)?he`

   d) `(T|t)*he`

Chapter 5

Typing it In

It is easy to take for granted the ability to enter, modify, and correct large amounts of text accurately and quickly, since most of us have some proficiency at it these days. But remember that, in the past, huge numbers of young people would go to secretarial school before they could work as typists or data entry clerks. The present generation may use computer or tablet keyboards from childhood, but those of us who remember having to learn to type as teenagers recall how hard it seemed at the time.

The development of the keyboard began before the computer, or course, for typewriters and similar equipment. And so, when computers were first developed, the best methods for text input were already known, requiring only slight alteration. In this chapter, we will look at the development of typing devices from the typewriter to the modern computer. We will also see methods for typing languages such as Chinese, where the number of characters might vastly outnumber the keys we could possibly place on a keyboard.

As early as the eighteenth century, work was beginning on devices for "automatic writing", but what we recognise today as a typewriter can be traced back to the first commercially successful examples, the work of the Pennsylvania-born newspaper editor Christopher Latham Scholes (1819–1890). His company was eventually sold to Remington & Sons, under whose brand typewriters were sold until the 1960s. The following pages show images from Scholes's early and more mature patent applications.

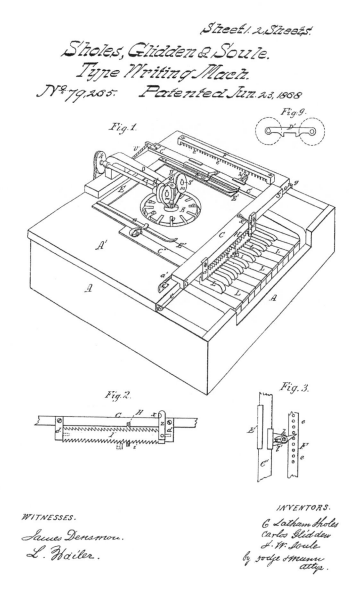

THE TYPE WRITING MACHINE OF C. L. SCHOLES, 1868 (FRONT VIEW). Unrecognisable as a modern typewriter, with piano-style keys and the paper held horizontally. Only a few units were produced commercially, before money ran out. Development on a new, more practical, design continued.

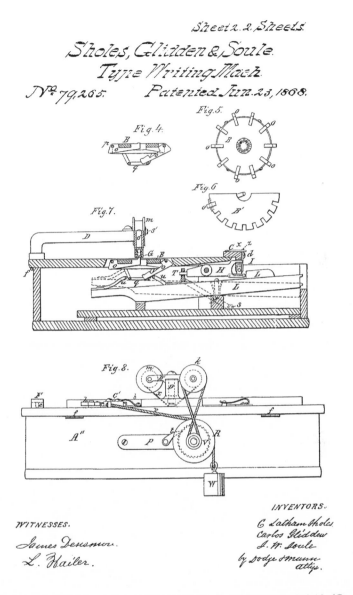

THE TYPE WRITING MACHINE OF C. L. SCHOLES, 1868 (SIDE VIEW). An early user of a demonstration machine, James Densmore, bought a 25% interest in the project, despite believing that it needed significant further development to be practical.

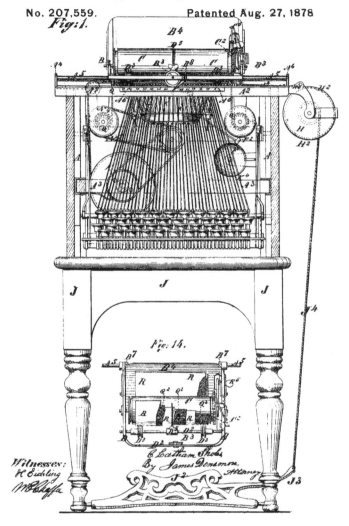

3 Sheets—Sheet 1

THE TYPE WRITING MACHINE OF C. L. SCHOLES, 1878 (FRONT VIEW). Rather more recognisable as a typewriter to modern eyes, with four rows of keys in roughly the same arrangement as computer keyboards today and the paper clipped into a rotating drum, allowing for secure and reliable placement of each row. There is a foot pedal for advancing to the next line.

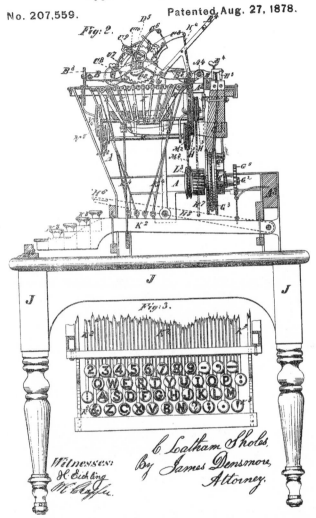

C. L. SHOLES.
Type-Writing Machine.

No. 207,559.   Patented Aug. 27, 1878.

Fig: 2.

Fig: 3.

Witnesses:
H. Eichling

C. Latham Sholes,
By James Densmore,
Attorney.

THE TYPE WRITING MACHINE OF C. L. SCHOLES, 1878 (SIDE VIEW AND KEYBOARD). You can see the key arrangement here. Note that there are no keys for 0 (zero) or 1 (one) since the keys for O (capital o) and I (capital i) were deemed similar enough – the machines were already complex, unreliable, and difficult and expensive to manufacture; anything which could reduce complexity was welcome.

This diagram shows the arrangement of "piano" keys on Scholes' first typewriter:

You can see that the alphabetic characters are largely in order. This caused mechanical problems with the machine. When a key was pressed, a *type-bar* with the correct letter would swing up to hit the paper. It would then fall back down by gravity. However, once a user became proficient and was hitting keys one after another in quick succession, the falling type-bar could rub against the next rising one, jamming, especially if the keys were next to one another in the row of type-bars. The keyboard was redesigned by analysing the English language to determine which letters commonly followed one another and moving them apart on the keyboard. This led to the QWERTY arrangement that is almost ubiquitous today. It also led to the urban myth that the QWERTY keyboard was intended to "slow the typist down because the machine could not cope". In fact, the rearrangement facilitated *faster* typing. Here is the keyboard layout from one of Scholes's later patents:

The most common (though still rather uncommon) alternative keyboard layout is the *Dvorak* layout, patented in 1936 by August Dvorak (1894–1975), a professor at the University of Washington. His layout, as specified in his patent, is shown on the opposite page. The layout has been modified slightly over the years by Dvorak and ANSI, the American National Standards Institute. The intent was to design, by scientific methods, a keyboard layout which is optimal for the human typing, irrespective of the demands of the machine being typed on. (We don't have to worry about jamming type-bars in the computer age.) The layout places the most common keys in the middle row, under the hands, the least common on the bottom row where it is most awkward to reach, and the keys are arranged left and right so that, commonly, key-presses alternate between the left and right hands in a rhythmic fashion. The layout has never caught on, however, though one can buy keyboards for most modern computers with the Dvorak layout, and it retains a band of admirers.

May 12, 1936. A. DVORAK ET AL **2,040,248**

TYPEWRITER KEYBOARD

Filed May 21, 1932

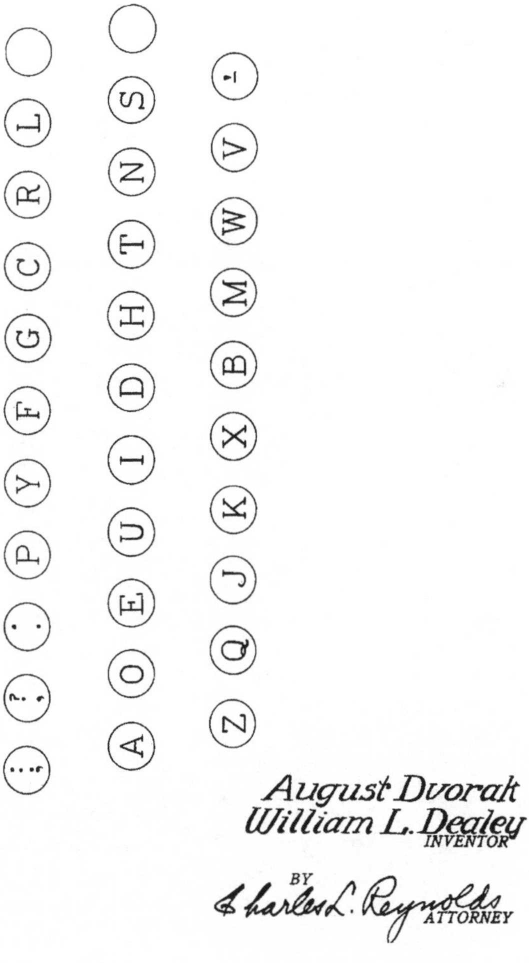

August Dvorak
William L. Dealey
INVENTOR

BY
Charles L. Reynolds
ATTORNEY

It is striking how similar the keyboards of these early typewriters are to those we use every day. Here is a keyboard from the early days of computing. It belongs to the UNIVAC system built by the Eckert-Mauchly Computer Corporation in 1953:

By the 1980s computer keyboards were almost identical in layout to today's, just rather larger and more solid. Here is an IBM Model M Keyboard from 1985:

The Author's own keyboard (Apple, 2015), with which this book was typed, is much the same, but very much thinner and lighter. Laptop keyboards must be smaller and thinner still.

What of languages other than English? We can divide them into three categories. First, those which use the so-called *Latin* alphabet (that is the familiar ABC...), but which contain characters with accents, or one or two extra characters only. Typically, these can be typed on a standard keyboard, using either modifier keys (holding down a key to make the next letter accented) or by using short sequences of keys (typing "`" followed by the "a" key for "à"). The second category is those languages, such as Modern Greek, which do not use the Latin alphabet, but whose alphabet has only a few tens of characters. These can be dealt with by using the same keyboard, simply with different letters printed on it. The last category is for languages such as Chinese. There are many tens of thousands of characters, and it is impractical to build a keyboard with that many keys, or to use one. Some system must be devised to allow all these characters to be typed on a limited number of keys. This is known as an *input system*.

One such input system in use in China, Singapore, and Taiwan is *Pinyin*. It requires knowing the pronunciation of the word: westernized spellings of the syllables are then used to find the right character. We shall write the word 櫻桃, which means cherry. In the Pinyin system, we type the western characters representing the sounds, and we are then are invited to disambiguate amongst the possibilities, as the word is formed. The word for cherry sounds like "ying" followed by "tao". First, we type "ying":

The computer displays a list of possibilities for the first character of our word. It does not yet know which syllable or syllables may follow. We choose the right one, and the computer replaces "ying" with the proper character.

Now, we type the second syllable "tao". We are again invited to choose a character from a list. We choose the correct one by clicking or typing a number, and the word is complete:

Another input method for Chinese is *Zhuyin*. This uses about 40 basic characters, which can be arranged on a normal computer keyboard like this:

The symbols are on the top-right of each key. These characters can be used to represent all sounds in the language. Just like Pinyin, the sounds lead to the characters. However, unlike Pinyin, there is no need for the user to know any western characters at all.

Let us type 櫻桃 using the Zhuyin system. We begin by typing one of the characters which represent sounds:

We continue to build the first character by typing the next Zhuyin symbol:

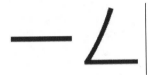

Now, we type in the *tone* using the number keys on the keyboard (there are four tones in Chinese, each a different variation on a given sound):

We can now see the full character, which replaces the Zhuyin ones we typed in. It is the wrong character, but do not worry – this will correct itself once the system knows the end of the word. We begin on the second character:

Now we type the second sound of the second character:

應ㄊㄠ

Again, we choose the tone. Contextual information, such as the previous character, is used to disambiguated the two-character sequence and, in this case, the most common possibility is correct:

櫻桃

Different systems are popular in each part of Asia, and in each generation, and depend upon the device in use. Indeed, one person may use a particular system on their computer and entirely another on their mobile phone, which has even less space for keys (real or virtual).

We have seen how English and the world's many other languages might be typed into the computer. There have been many attempts to replace the keyboard for text input, such as voice recognition, which have made some inroads in automotive and niche applications, but for general purpose computing, the keyboard, real or virtual, is still king.

Chapter 6

Saving Space

As computers get ever faster, we ask ever more of them: a higher-resolution film streamed in real time, a faster download, or the same experience on a mobile device over a slow connection as we have at home or in the office over a fast one. When we talk of efficiency, we are concerned with the time taken to do a task, the space required to store data, and knock-on effects such as how often we have to charge our device's battery. And so we cannot simply say "things are getting faster all the time: we need not worry about efficiency."

An important tool for reducing the space information takes up (and so, increasing the speed with which it can be moved around) is *compression*. The idea is to process the information in such as way that it becomes smaller, but also so that it may be *decompressed* – that is to say, the process must be reversible.

Imagine we want to send a coffee order. Instead of writing "Four espressos, two double espressos, a cappuccino, and two lattes", we might write "4E2DC2L". This relies, of course, on the person to whom we are sending the order knowing how to decompress it. The instructions for decompressing might be longer than the message itself, but if we are sending similar messages each day, we need only share the instructions once. We have reduced the message from 67 characters to 7, making it almost ten times smaller.

This sort of compression happens routinely, and it is really just a matter of choosing a better representation for storing a particular kind of information. It tends to be more successful the more uniform the data is. Can we come up with a compression method which works for any data? If not, what about one which works well for a whole class of data, such as text in the English language, or photographs, or video?

First, we should address the question of whether or not this kind of universal compression is even possible. Imagine that our message is just one character long, and our alphabet (our set of possible characters) is the familiar A,B,C...Z. There are then exactly 26 different possible messages, each consisting of a single character. Assuming each message is equally likely, there is no way to reduce the length of messages, and so compress them. In fact, this is not entirely true: we can make a tiny improvement – we could send the empty message for, say, A, and then one out of twenty-six messages would be smaller. What about a message of length two? Again, if all messages are equally likely, we can do no better: if we were to encode some of the two-letter sequences using just one letter, we would have to use two-letter sequences to indicate the one-letter ones – we would have gained nothing. The same argument applies for sequences of length three or four or five or indeed of any length.

However, all is not lost. Most information has patterns in it, or elements which are more or less common. For example, most of the words in this book can be found in an English dictionary. When there are patterns, we can reserve our shorter codes for the most common sequences, reducing the overall length of the message. It is not immediately apparent how to go about this, so we shall proceed by example. Consider the following text:

> Whether it was embarrassment or impatience, the
> judge rocked backwards and forwards on his seat.
> The man behind him, whom he had been talking
> with earlier, leant forward again, either to give him
> a few general words of encouragement or some
> specific piece of advice. Below them in the hall the
> people talked to each other quietly but animatedly.
> The two factions had earlier seemed to hold views
> strongly opposed to each other but now they began to
> intermingle, a few individuals pointed up at K., others
> pointed at the judge. The air in the room was fuggy
> and extremely oppressive, those who were standing
> furthest away could hardly even be seen through it.
> It must have been especially troublesome for those
> visitors who were in the gallery, as they were forced
> to quietly ask the participants in the assembly what
> exactly was happening, albeit with timid glances at

the judge. The replies they received were just as quiet,
and given behind the protection of a raised hand.

We shall take as our dictionary the 100 most commonly-used
English words of three or more letters:

00	the	25	there	50	two	75	part
01	and	26	use	51	more	76	over
02	you	27	each	52	write	77	new
03	that	28	which	53	see	78	sound
04	was	29	she	54	number	79	take
05	for	30	how	55	way	80	only
06	are	31	their	56	could	81	little
07	with	32	will	57	people	82	work
08	his	33	other	58	than	83	know
09	they	34	about	59	first	84	place
10	this	35	out	60	water	85	year
11	have	36	many	61	been	86	live
12	from	37	then	62	call	87	back
13	one	38	them	63	who	88	give
14	had	39	these	64	its	89	most
15	word	40	some	65	now	90	very
16	but	41	her	66	find	91	after
17	not	42	would	67	long	92	thing
18	what	43	make	68	down	93	our
19	all	44	like	69	day	94	just
20	were	45	him	70	did	95	name
21	when	46	into	71	get	96	good
22	your	47	time	72	come	97	sentence
23	can	48	has	73	made	98	man
24	said	49	look	74	may	99	think

These words will be compressed by representing them as the
two-character sequences 00, 01, 02, . . . , 97, 98, 99. We don't bother
with the one and two letter words, common though they are, because they are already as short or shorter than our codes. We
assume our text does not contain digits, so that any digit sequence
may be interpreted as a code. Any word, text, or punctuation not
in the word list will be rendered literally. If we substitute these
codes into our text, we find a somewhat underwhelming level of

compression:

> Whether it 04 embarrassment or impatience, 00 judge
> rocked backwards 01 forwards on 08 seat. The 98
> behind 45, whom he 14 61 talking 07 earlier, leant
> forward again, either to 88 45 a few general 15s of
> encouragement or 40 specific piece of advice. Below
> 38 in 00 hall 00 people talked to 27 33 quietly 16
> animatedly. The 50 factions 14 earlier seemed to
> views strongly opposed to 27 33 16 65 09 began to
> intermingle, a few individuals pointed up to K., 33s
> pointed at 00 judge. The air in 00 room 04 fuggy 01
> extremely oppressive, those 63 20 standing furthest
> away could hardly ever be 53n through it. It must 11
> 61 especially troublesome 05 those visitors 63 20 in 00
> gallery, as 09 20 forced to quietly ask 00 participants in
> 00 assembly 18 exactly 04 happening, albeit 07 timid
> glances at 00 judge. The replies 09 received 20 94 as
> quiet, 01 given behind 00 protection of a raised hand.

The original text had 975 characters; the new one has 891. One
more small change can be made – where there is a sequence of codes,
we can squash them together if they have only spaces between them
in the source:

> Whether it 04 embarrassment or impatience, 00
> judge rocked backwards 01 forwards on 08 seat.
> The 98 behind 45, whom he 1461 talking 07 earlier,
> leant forward again, either to 8845 a few general
> 15s of encouragement or 40 specific piece of advice.
> Below 38 in 00 hall 00 people talked to 2733 quietly
> 16 animatedly. The 50 factions 14 earlier seemed
> to views strongly opposed to 2733166509 began to
> intermingle, a few individuals pointed up to K., 33s
> pointed at 00 judge. The air in 00 room 04 fuggy 01
> extremely oppressive, those 6320 standing furthest
> away could hardly ever be 53n through it. It must 11
> 61 especially troublesome 05 those visitors 6320 in 00
> gallery, as 0920 forced to quietly ask 00 participants in
> 00 assembly 18 exactly 04 happening, albeit 07 timid
> glances at 00 judge. The replies 09 received 2094 as
> quiet, 01 given behind 00 protection of a raised hand.

We are down to 880 characters, a reduction of about 10% compared with the original. The top 100 words in English are known to cover about half of the printed words, in general. We have not quite achieved that in this example.

Let us try counting the number of each character in our text to see if we can take advantage of the fact that some letters are more common than others (our current method makes no use of the fact that, for example, spaces are very common):

167	*space*	30	l	10	,
120	e	24	w	8	.
71	t	19	p	5	k
62	a	19	m	4	j
55	i	19	g	4	T
51	h	19	c	3	q
49	o	18	u	2	x
45	r	15	y	1	W
42	n	13	f	1	K
41	s	13	b	1	I
33	d	10	v	1	B

The space character is by far the most common (we say it has the highest frequency). The frequencies of the lower case letters are roughly what we might expect from recalling the value of Scrabble tiles, the punctuation characters are infrequent, and the capital letters very infrequent.

We have talked about what a bit is, how 8 bits make a byte, and how one byte is sufficient to store a character (at least in English). Our original message is 975 bytes, or $975 \times 8 = 7800$ bits. We could encode each of the 33 characters we have found in our text using a different pattern of 6 bits, since 33 is less than 64, which is the number of 6-bit combinations 000000,000001,...,111110,111111. (The number of 5-bit combinations is 32, which is not quite enough.) This would reduce our space to $975 \times 6 = 5850$ bits. However, we would have wasted much of the possible set of codes and taken no advantage of our knowledge of how frequently each character occurs. What we should like is a code which uses shorter bit patterns for more common characters, and longer bit patterns for less common ones. Let us write out the beginnings of such a code:

space	0
e	1

t	00
a	01
i	10
h	11
o	000
⋮	⋮

There is a problem, though. It is very easy to encode a word; for example, "heat" encodes as 1110100 (that is, 11 for "h", 1 for "e", 01 for "a", and 00 for "t"). However, we can decode it in many different ways. The sequence 1110100 might equally be taken to mean "eee*space*e*space*" or "hii*space*". Our code is ambiguous. What we require is a code with the so-called *prefix property* – that is, arranged such that no code in the table is a prefix of another. For example, we cannot have both 001 and 0010 as codes, since 001 appears at the beginning of 0010. This property allows for unambiguous decoding. Consider the following alternative code:

space	00
e	010
t	011
a	100
i	101
h	110
o	111
⋮	⋮

This code is unambiguous – no code is a prefix of another. The word "heat" encodes as 110010100011 and may be decoded unambiguously. We can have the computer automatically create an appropriate code for our text, taking into account the frequencies. Then, by sending the code table along with the text, we ensure it may be unambiguously decoded. Here is the full table of unambiguous codes for the frequencies derived from our text:

space	111	l	10100	,	000100
e	100	w	00011	.	0101101
t	1011	p	110101	k	11000011
a	0111	m	110100	j	11000001
i	0110	g	110011	T	11000000

h	0100	c	110010	q	01011001
o	0011	u	110001	x	110000100
r	0010	y	010111	W	010110001
n	0000	f	010101	K	010110000
s	11011	b	010100	I	1100001011
d	10101	v	000101	B	1100001010

The information in this table can, alternatively, be viewed as a diagram:

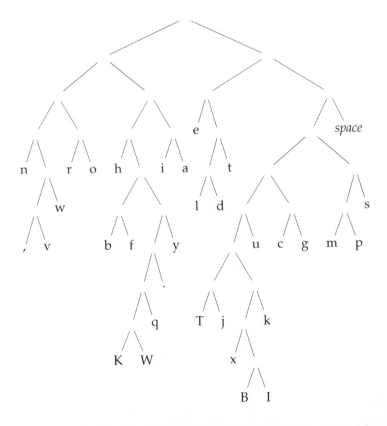

In order to find the code for a letter, we start at the top, adding 0 each time we go left and 1 each time we go right. For example, we can see that the code for the letter "g" is Right Right Left Left Right Right or 110011. You can see that all the letters are at the bottom edge of the diagram, a visual reinforcement of the prefix property. The compressed message length for our example text is 4171 bits, or 522 bytes, about half of the original message length. Sending the tree requires another 197 bits, or 25 bytes. (We do not discuss the method here.) Of course, the longer the message, the less it matters, since the message will be so big by comparison. These codes are called *Huffman codes*, named after David A. Huffman, who invented them whilst a PhD student at MIT in the 1950s.

A common use for this sort of encoding is in the sending of faxes. A fax consists of a high-resolution black and white image. In this case, we are not compressing characters, but the black and white image of those characters itself. Take the following fragment:

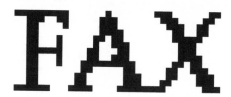

This image is 37 pixels wide and 15 tall. Here it is with a grid superimposed to make it easier to count pixels:

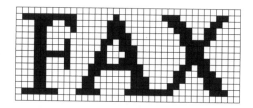

We cannot compress the whole thing with Huffman encoding, since we do not know the frequencies at the outset – a fax is sent incrementally. One machine scans the document whilst the machine at the other end of the phone line prints the result as it pulls paper from its roll. It had to be this way because, when fax machines were in their infancy, computer memory was very expensive, so receiving and storing the whole image in one go and only then printing it out was not practical.

The solution the fax system uses is as follows. Instead of sending individual pixels, we send, a line at a time, a list of *runs*. Each run is a length of white pixels or a length of black pixels. For example, a line of width 39 might contain 12 pixels of white, then 4 of black, then 2 of white, then 18 of black, and then 3 of white. We look up the code for each run and send the codes in order. To avoid the problem of having to gather frequency data for the whole page, a pre-prepared master code table is used, upon which everyone agrees. The table has been built by gathering frequencies from thousands of text documents in several languages and typefaces, and then collating the frequencies of the various black and white runs.

Here is the table of codes for black and white runs of lengths 0 to 63. (We need length 0 because a line is always assumed to begin white, and a zero-length white run is required if the line actually begins black.)

Run	White	Black	Run	White	Black
0	00110101	0000110111	32	00011011	000001101010
1	0000111	010	33	00010010	000001101011
2	0111	11	34	00010011	000011010010
3	1000	10	35	00010100	000011010011
4	1011	011	36	00010101	000011010100
5	1100	0011	37	00010110	000011010101
6	1110	0010	38	00010111	000011010110
7	1111	00011	39	00101000	000011010111
8	1011	000101	40	00101001	000001101100
9	10100	000100	41	00101010	000001101101
10	00111	0000100	42	00101011	000011011010
11	01000	0000101	43	00101100	000011011011
12	001000	0000111	44	00101101	000001010100
13	000011	00000100	45	00000100	000001010101
14	110100	00000111	46	00000101	000001010110
15	110101	000011000	47	00001010	000001010111
16	101010	0000010111	48	0000101	00001100100
17	101011	0000011000	49	01010010	000001100101
18	0100111	0000001000	50	01010011	000001010010
19	0001100	00001100111	51	01010100	000001010011
20	0001000	00001101000	52	01010101	000000100100
21	0010111	00001101100	53	00100100	000000110111
22	00000011	00000110111	54	00100101	000000111000
23	0000100	00000101000	55	01011000	000000100111
24	0101000	00000010111	56	01011001	000000101000
25	0101011	00000011000	57	01011010	000001011000
26	0010011	000011001010	58	01011011	000001011001
27	0100100	000011001011	59	01001010	000000101011

28	0011000	000011001100	60	00110010	000000101100
29	00000010	000011001101	61	00110010	000001011010
30	00000011	000001101000	62	00110011	000001100110
31	00011010	000001101001	63	00110100	000001100111

Notice that the prefix property applies only to alternating black and white codes. There is never a black code followed by a black code or a white code followed by a white code. The shortest codes are reserved for the most common runs – the black ones of length two and three. We can write out the codes for the first two lines of our image by counting the pixels manually:

Run length	Colour	Bit pattern	Pattern length
37	white	00010110	8
1	white	0000111	7
9	black	000100	6
6	white	1110	4
1	black	010	3
7	white	1111	4
3	black	10	2
6	white	1110	4
2	white	0111	4

So we transmit the bit pattern 00010110 0000111 000100 1110 010 1111 10 1110 0111. The number of bits required to transmit the image has dropped from $37 \times 2 = 74$ to $8 + 7 + 6 + 4 + 3 + 4 + 2 + 4 + 2 + 4 = 46$. Due to the preponderance of white space in written text (blank lines, spaces between words, and page margins), faxes can often be compressed to less than twenty per cent of their original size. Modern fax systems which take advantage of the fact that successive lines are often similar can reduce this to five per cent.

Of course, we often want more than just black and white. (Even black and white television was not really just black and white – there were shades of grey.) How can we compress grey and colour photographic images? The reversible (lossless) compression we have used so far tends not to work well, so we look at methods which do not retain all the information in an image. This is known as lossy compression. One option is simply to use fewer colours. Figure A on page 76 shows a picture reduced from the original to 64, then 8, then 2 greys. We see a marked decrease in size, but the quality reduces rapidly. On the printed page, we can certainly see that 8 and 2 greys are too few, but 64 seems alright. On a computer screen, you would see that even 64 is a noticeable decrease in quality.

If we can't reduce the number of greys with a satisfactory result, what about the resolution? Let us try discarding one out of every two pixels in each row of the original, and one out of every two pixels in each column. Then we will go further and discard three from every four, and finally seven from every eight. The result is Figure B. In these examples, we removed some information and then scaled up the image again when printing it on the page. Again, the first reduction is not too bad – at least at the printed size of this book. The 3/4 is a little obvious, and the 7/8 is dreadful. Algorithms have been devised which can take the images which have had data discarded like those above and, when scaling them back to normal size, attempt to smooth the image. This will reduce the "blocky" look, but it can lead to indistinctness. Figure C shows the same images as Figure B, displayed using a modern smoothing method.

Finally, Figure D shows the images compressed using an algorithm especially intended for photographic use, the JPEG (Joint Photographic Experts Group) algorithm, first conceived in the 1980s. At "75% quality", the image is down to nineteen per cent of its original size and almost indistinguishable from the original.

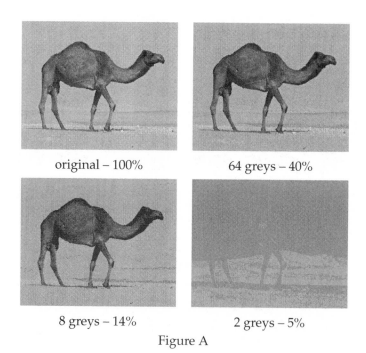

original – 100%   64 greys – 40%

8 greys – 14%   2 greys – 5%

Figure A

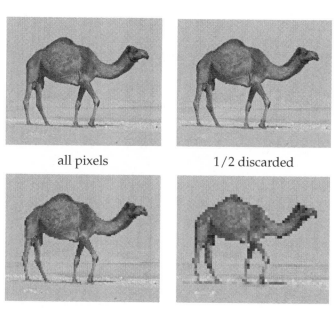

all pixels   1/2 discarded

3/4 discarded   7/8 discarded

Figure B

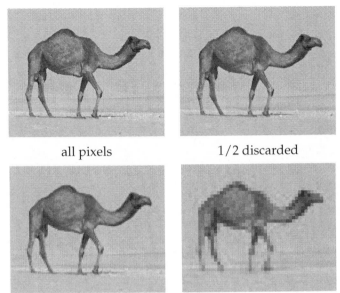

all pixels | 1/2 discarded

3/4 discarded | 7/8 discarded

Figure C

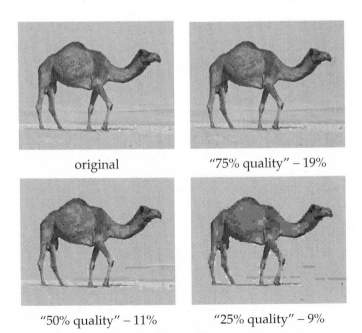

original | "75% quality" – 19%

"50% quality" – 11% | "25% quality" – 9%

Figure D

Problems

Solutions on page 154.

1. Count the frequencies of the characters in this piece of text
   and assign them to the Huffman codes, filling in the following
   table. Then encode the text up to "more lightly.".

   > 'I have a theory which I suspect is rather
   > immoral,' Smiley went on, more lightly. 'Each of us
   > has only a quantum of compassion. That if we
   > lavish our concern on every stray cat, we never get
   > to the centre of things.'

Letter	Frequency	Code	Letter	Frequency	Code
		111			110100
		100			110011
		1011			110010
		0111			110001
		0110			010111
		0100			010101
		0011			01010000
		0010			01010001
		0000			01010010
		11011			01010011
		10101			01011000
		10100			01011001
		00011			01011010
		110101			01011011

2. Consider the following frequency table and text. Decode it.

Letter	Frequency	Code	Letter	Frequency	Code
space	20	111	s	2	00011
e	12	100	d	2	110101
t	9	1011	T	1	110100
h	7	0111	n	1	110011
o	7	0110	w	1	110010
m	6	0100	p	1	110001
r	5	0011	b	1	010111

a	4	0010	l	1	010101
f	4	0000	v	1	01010000
c	4	11011	y	1	01010001
u	4	10101	.	1	01010010
i	3	10100			

```
1101000111100001110011100100011100111010001100100
1001100110110001111111001001111010011011011111100
1000111001110100001011010110011110101110001111011
0000001110110110011011101001010101110110111111000
1101110101000000001110000011000111110110111100010
0111011011011101011110001010110100010100001001101
0111100101011111101101111001111011101000100100111
1011011110001010001111011011011110111010100110101
0010
```

3. Encode the following fax image. There is no need to use zero-length white runs at the beginning of lines starting with a black pixel.

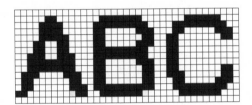

4. Decode the following fax image to the same 37x15 grid. There are no zero-length white runs at the beginning of lines starting with a black pixel.

```
0001011000001110001111110001110000011100000011001
0110000100100000010001111111001010001011001001111
1110010000011111110110101110111111101111111011000
0111111100100111111011110111111110010000011100010
1000111011110111000100011100010010001110111101110
0010001111111001001111110111101111111001000001111
1111011011111101111011111111101100001111111011011
1101110100111111110110000111111110110111011110011
1000111110110000111000010010000000100100000010001
1100001110001111110010111000101011000010110
```

Chapter 7

Doing Sums

How do we calculate the answer to $1 + 2 \times 3$? In our heads, perhaps, or on paper. But how do we decide which operation to do first (the $+$ or the $\times$?) Well, in mathematics, we have the convention that, in this situation, the multiplication goes first. So we may work as follows:

$$1 + \underline{2 \times 3}$$
$$\implies \quad \underline{1 + 6}$$
$$\implies \quad 7$$

Something like $1 + 2 \times 3$ is an example of a mathematical *expression*. (We have underlined the part of the expression being worked on at each stage.) Rewriting it stage by stage, making it smaller each time, until we reach a final answer, is called *evaluating* the expression. The result is a *value*, which is an expression that can be reduced no further: 7 is just 7. We could rewrite it as $3 + 4$ or $1 + 1 + 5$, of course, but we like each subsequent expression to be simpler than the last. Computer programs often involve these kind of expressions, and indeed in some programming languages, the whole program is just one big expression.

It would be simpler if we could represent such expressions in an unambiguous way, so that we don't need to think about the rules for which operations happen in which order. (It's simple in our example, but expressions in computer programs can be huge.) We can just add parentheses to the expression: $1 + (2 \times 3)$. Now the rule for choosing what to do next can be stated more simply: evaluate a part of the expression which contains no parentheses first.

Note that for this to work, we have to parenthesise even expressions
where the parentheses cannot affect the result, for example $1 + (2 + (3 + 4))$.

It can be difficult for humans to read such over-parenthesised expressions (which is why mathematicians use the minimum number
of parentheses and rely on a set of ad-hoc rules for disambiguation
– the insistence on explicit preciseness can actually be antithetical to
doing mathematics). For computers, however, this representation
is ideal. We can see the structure of these expressions more clearly
by drawing them like this:

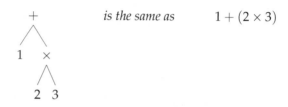

These are called *trees*, because they have a branching structure.
Unlike real trees, we draw them upside-down, with the *root* at the
top. We can show the steps of evaluation, just as before, without
the need for any parentheses:

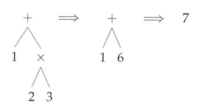

In fact, this is the representation a computer would use inter-
nally (not literal drawings, of course, but a structure of this form
in its memory). When we type in a computer program using the
keyboard, we might write $1 + 2 * 3$. (There is no $\times$ key on the
keyboard.) It will be converted into tree form and can then be
evaluated automatically, and quickly, by the computer.

When we write instructions for computers, we want a single set
of instructions to work for any given input. To do this, we write our
expressions – just like in maths – to use quantities like x and y and

so on. These quantities are not fixed, but can be different each time. We call them *variables*. For example, here is an expression which calculates the cube of a given number x:

When we evaluate this in an environment in which $x = 4$, we get one result:

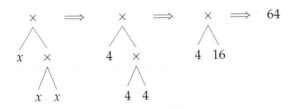

When we evaluate it, instead, in an environment in which $x = 50$, we get another:

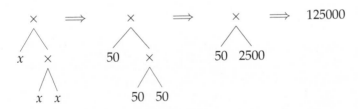

Of course, we can write the same thing out on a single line, and evaluate it without drawing the tree explicitly:

$$
\begin{aligned}
& x \times x \times x \\
\Longrightarrow\ & 50 \times \underline{50 \times 50} \\
\Longrightarrow\ & 50 \times \underline{2500} \\
\Longrightarrow\ & 125000
\end{aligned}
$$

When evaluating $x \times x \times x$, the result of the computation doesn't rely on the order in which we evaluate it: we can do $(x \times x) \times x$ or $x \times (x \times x)$. However, computers like to follow rules exactly, so typically the order is chosen when the expression is read into the computer, either leftmost-first or rightmost-first.

An expression like this, which depends on the value of a variable, is called a *function*. In this case, we've written a function which finds the cube of a number. So, let's name it:

$$\text{cube } x = x \times x \times x$$

Now, we can give the value of x explicitly, writing it out like this:

$$
\begin{array}{rl}
& \underline{\text{cube } 50} \\
\Longrightarrow & \underline{50 \times 50} \times 50 \\
\Longrightarrow & \underline{50 \times 2500} \\
\Longrightarrow & 125000
\end{array}
$$

In the first step, we substituted cube 50 with its definition. We can view the computation in tree form too:

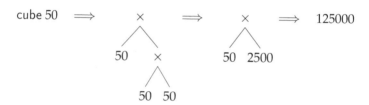

Let's introduce some more interesting operators in our expressions. We will introduce the $=$ or equals operator, and the special values *true* and *false* (not every value has to be a number). Now, we can write $x = 4$, and, if x is indeed 4 in the current environment, we get *true*; otherwise, we get *false*. Here, $=$ is the operator, and x and 4 are the *operands*. In the expression $1 + 2$ the operator is $+$, and the operands are 1 and 2.

Now, we can build a more complicated operator which can make a decision between two sub-expressions based on an equality test like this. For example, we may write:

$$\text{if } x = 4 \text{ then } 0 \text{ else } x + 1$$

(This is only somewhat related to the if...then...else construct of Chapter 4 – please put it out of your mind.) As a mathematical construct, this looks rather strange: we are used to seeing operators like $+$ and $\times$, which consist of one symbol and have an operand either side. This new operator has three parts (if, then, and else) and three operands ($x = 4, 0$, and $x + 1$), and they are spread all over the place! But if we write it out as a tree, it looks much like the earlier trees:

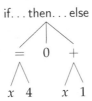

An operator having more than two operands is not so strange after all. Suppose we evaluate it in the environment where $x = 6$:

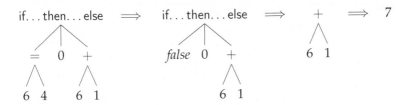

Of course, we can write this out in linear form:

$$\text{if } \underline{6 = 4} \text{ then } 0 \text{ else } 6 + 1$$
$$\implies \text{if } \textit{false} \text{ then } 0 \text{ else } 6 + 1$$
$$\implies \underline{6 + 1}$$
$$\implies 7$$

And, we can name the function:

$$\text{test } l =$$
$$\text{if } x = 4 \text{ then } 0 \text{ else } x + 1$$

We are getting a little closer to the sorts of calculations a real program does: making decisions about which part of an expression to evaluate based on input data and defining and using reusable functions.

Now let us write a real, useful function. Given a number, such as 4, it will calculate the *factorial*, written 4!, of the number. The factorial of a number is all the numbers from 1 to that number multiplied together. For example, the factorial of 4 is $4 \times 3 \times 2 \times 1$, which is 24. The number of possible orderings of a pack of playing cards is 52!, which is a very large number indeed. To calculate a factorial, we start at the given number, and we want to keep multiplying it by the number one smaller and one smaller and one smaller, until we reach 1. Then, we want to stop, rather than keep multiplying by 0, -1, -2 etc. You can see that we will have to use an if ... then ... else construct because we have a decision to make. Let us begin to define our function. The first part is easy – if the number is 1, the answer is 1:

$$\text{factorial } n =$$
$$\text{if } n = 1 \text{ then } 1 \text{ else } \ldots$$

Now we must consider what to do when the number is greater than 1. In this case, we want to multiply the number by the factorial of the number one smaller since, for example, $4 \times 3 \times 2 \times 1 = 4 \times 3!$ So we write it out:

$$\text{factorial } n =$$
$$\text{if } n = 1 \text{ then } 1 \text{ else } n \times \text{factorial } (n - 1)$$

Notice that our function uses itself within its own definition. This is not a problem as long as the computation eventually completes and gives a result. Here it is for the number 4:

$$\begin{aligned}
&\underline{\text{factorial } 4} \\
\Longrightarrow\quad &\text{if } \underline{4 = 1} \text{ then } 1 \text{ else } 4 \times \text{factorial } (4 - 1) \\
\Longrightarrow\quad &\underline{\text{if } \textit{false} \text{ then } 1 \text{ else } 4 \times \text{factorial } (4 - 1)} \\
\Longrightarrow\quad &4 \times \text{factorial } \underline{(4 - 1)} \\
\Longrightarrow\quad &4 \times \underline{\text{factorial } 3} \\
\Longrightarrow\quad &4 \times (\text{if } \underline{3 = 1} \text{ then } 1 \text{ else } 3 \times \text{factorial } (3 - 1)) \\
\Longrightarrow\quad &4 \times (\underline{\text{if } \textit{false} \text{ then } 1 \text{ else } 3 \times \text{factorial } (3 - 1)}) \\
\Longrightarrow\quad &4 \times (3 \times \text{factorial } \underline{(3 - 1)}) \\
\Longrightarrow\quad &4 \times (3 \times \underline{\text{factorial } 2}) \\
\Longrightarrow\quad &4 \times (3 \times (\text{if } \underline{2 = 1} \text{ then } 1 \text{ else } 2 \times \text{factorial } (2 - 1)))
\end{aligned}$$

$\Longrightarrow$ $4 \times (3 \times ($if *false* then 1 else $2 \times$ factorial $(2-1)))$

$\Longrightarrow$ $4 \times (3 \times (2 \times$ factorial $(\underline{2-1})))$

$\Longrightarrow$ $4 \times (3 \times (2 \times \underline{\text{factorial } 1}))$

$\Longrightarrow$ $4 \times (3 \times (2 \times ($if $\underline{1=1}$ then 1 else $2 \times$ factorial $(1-1))))$

$\Longrightarrow$ $4 \times (3 \times (2 \times ($if *true* then 1 else $2 \times$ factorial $(1-1))))$

$\Longrightarrow$ $4 \times (3 \times (\underline{2 \times 1}))$

$\Longrightarrow$ $4 \times (\underline{3 \times 2})$

$\Longrightarrow$ $\underline{4 \times 6}$

$\Longrightarrow$ 24

We said earlier that we wanted the expression to get smaller each step. This isn't the case here: we relax this restriction to say simply that in a properly working program with a proper input, the computation eventually finishes. Here is the tree for factorial:

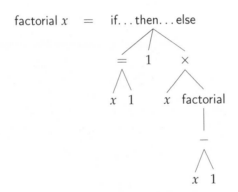

Consider another simple task with numbers. Given two numbers x and y, we wish to calculate x^y, which is pronounced "x to the power y". This is equal to x multiplied by itself y times. So, for example, $2^5 = 2 \times 2 \times 2 \times 2 \times 2 = 32$. On the other hand, $5^2 = 5 \times 5 = 25$. Note that it is a mathematical convention that any number to the power 0 is 1. This fact allows us to begin to write the power function (notice it has two inputs):

$$\text{power } x\ y =$$
$$\text{if } y = 0 \text{ then } 1 \text{ else} \ldots$$

If y is greater than 0, on the other hand, we want to calculate x times x^{y-1}:

> power $x\ y =$
> > if $y = 0$ then 1 else $x\ \times$ power $x\ (y - 1)$

So, we can now calculate 2^5, showing just the important steps:

$$\text{power } 2\ 5$$
$\Longrightarrow\quad 2 \times \text{power } 2\ 4$
$\Longrightarrow\quad 2 \times (2 \times \text{power } 2\ 3)$
$\Longrightarrow\quad 2 \times (2 \times (2 \times \text{power } 2\ 2))$
$\Longrightarrow\quad 2 \times (2 \times (2 \times (2 \times \text{power } 2\ 1)))$
$\Longrightarrow\quad 2 \times (2 \times (2 \times (2 \times (2 \times \text{power } 2\ 0))))$
$\Longrightarrow\quad 2 \times (2 \times (2 \times (2 \times (2 \times 1))))$
$\Longrightarrow\quad 32$

We have looked at numbers like 2 and 32, and the truth values *true* and *false*, but interesting programs often have to operate on more complicated structures. One such is a *list*, which we write with square brackets and commas, like this: [1, 5, 4]. A list is an ordered collection of other values. That is to say, the lists [1, 5, 4] and [5, 4, 1] are different, even though they contain the same values. There is an empty list [] which contains no items. The first element of a list is called the *head*, and there is a built-in function to get at it:

$$\text{head } [1, 5, 4]$$
$\Longrightarrow\quad 1$

The rest of the elements are collectively referred to as the *tail*, and again there is a built-in function to retrieve it:

$$\text{tail } [1, 5, 4]$$
$\Longrightarrow\quad [5, 4]$

The empty list [] has neither a head nor a tail. We need just one more thing for our example programs, and that is the • operator which sticks two lists together:

$$[1, 5, 4] \bullet [2, 3]$$
$\Longrightarrow\quad [1, 5, 4, 2, 3]$

Let us write a function to find the length of a list using the tail function:

$$\text{length } l =$$
$$\text{if } l = [] \text{ then } 0 \text{ else } 1 + \text{length (tail } l)$$

The empty list has length 0, and the length of any other list is 1 plus the length of its tail. Notice that the $=$ operator works on lists too. We can try a sample evaluation:

$$\text{length } [2,3]$$
$\Longrightarrow$ if $[2,3] = []$ then 0 else $1 + \text{length (tail } [2,3])$
$\Longrightarrow$ if *false* then 0 else $1 + \text{length (tail } [2,3])$
$\Longrightarrow$ $1 + \text{length (tail } [2,3])$
$\Longrightarrow$ $1 + \text{length } [3]$
$\Longrightarrow$ $1 + \text{if } [3] = []$ then 0 else $1 + \text{length (tail } [3])$
$\Longrightarrow$ $1 + \text{if } \textit{false}$ then 0 else $1 + \text{length (tail } [3])$
$\Longrightarrow$ $1 + (1 + \text{length (tail } [3]))$
$\Longrightarrow$ $1 + (1 + \text{length } [])$
$\Longrightarrow$ $1 + (1 + \text{if } [] = []$ then 0 else $1 + \text{length (tail } l))$
$\Longrightarrow$ $1 + (1 + \text{if } \textit{false}$ then 0 else $1 + \text{length (tail } l))$
$\Longrightarrow$ $1 + (1 + 0)$
$\Longrightarrow$ $1 + 1$
$\Longrightarrow$ 2

These diagrams are becoming a little unwieldy, so as we write more complicated functions, we will leave some of the detail out, concentrating on the repeated uses of the main function we are writing, here length:

$$\text{length } [2,3]$$
$\Longrightarrow$ $1 + \text{length } [3]$
$\Longrightarrow$ $1 + (1 + \text{length } [])$
$\Longrightarrow$ $1 + (1 + 0)$
$\Longrightarrow$ 2

Much better. We can modify our function easily to calculate the sum of a list of numbers:

sum $l =$
  if $l = []$ then 0 else head $l +$ sum (tail l)

$$\begin{array}{rl} & \text{sum } [9, 1, 302] \\ \Longrightarrow & 9 + \text{sum } [1, 302] \\ \Longrightarrow & 9 + (1 + \text{sum } [302]) \\ \Longrightarrow & 9 + (1 + (302 + \text{sum } [])) \\ \Longrightarrow & 9 + (1 + (302 + 0)) \\ \Longrightarrow & 312 \end{array}$$

Time for something a little more ambitious. How may we reverse a list? For example, we want reverse $[1, 3, 5, 7]$ to give $[7, 5, 3, 1]$. Remember that we only have access to the first element of a list (the head), and the list which itself forms the tail of a given list – we do not have a direct way to access the end of the list. This prevents us from simply repeatedly taking the last element of the list and building a new one with the • operator (which, you recall, sticks two lists together). Well, we can at least write out the part for the empty list, since reversing the empty list just gives the empty list:

reverse $l =$
  if $l = []$ then $[]$ else $\ldots$

If the list is not empty, it has a head and a tail. We want to make the head go at the end of the final list, and before that, we want the rest of the list, itself reversed. So we write:

reverse $l =$
  if $l = []$ then $[]$ else [head l] • reverse (tail l)

Notice that we wrote [head l] rather than just head l because we need to turn it into a list so that the • operator can work. Let us check that it works (again, in our shortened form of diagram):

$$\frac{reverse\ [1,2,3]}{}$$
$$\Longrightarrow \quad reverse\ [2,3] \bullet [1]$$
$$\Longrightarrow \quad (reverse\ [3] \bullet [2]) \bullet [1]$$
$$\Longrightarrow \quad (([3] \bullet reverse\ []) \bullet [2]) \bullet [1]$$
$$\Longrightarrow \quad (([3] \bullet []) \bullet [2]) \bullet [1]$$
$$\Longrightarrow \quad [3,2,1]$$

Let us approach a more complicated problem. How might we sort a list into numerical order, whatever order it is in to start with? For example, we want to sort [53, 9, 2, 6, 19] to produce [2, 6, 9, 19, 53]. The problem is a little unapproachable – it seems rather complex. One way to begin is to see if we can solve the simplest part of the problem. Well just like for reverse, sorting a list of length zero is easy – there is nothing to do:

sort $l =$
  if $l = []$ then $[]$ else ...

If the list has length greater than zero, it has a head and a tail. Assume for a moment that the tail is already sorted – then we just need to insert the head into the tail at the correct position and the whole list will be sorted. Here is a definition for sort, assuming we have an insert function (we shall concoct insert in a moment):

sort $l =$
  if $l = []$ then $[]$ else insert (head l) (sort (tail l))

If the list is empty, we do nothing; otherwise, we insert the head of the list into its sorted tail. Assuming insert exists, here is the whole evaluation of our sorting procedure on the list [53, 9, 2, 6, 19], showing only uses of sort and insert for brevity:

$$\frac{sort\ [53,9,2,6,19]}{}$$
$$\Longrightarrow \quad insert\ 53\ (sort\ [9,2,6,19])$$
$$\Longrightarrow \quad insert\ 53\ (insert\ 9\ (sort\ [2,6,19]))$$
$$\Longrightarrow \quad insert\ 53\ (insert\ 9\ (insert\ 2\ (sort\ [6,19])))$$
$$\Longrightarrow \quad insert\ 53\ (insert\ 9\ (insert\ 2\ (insert\ 6\ (sort\ [19]))))$$

$\Longrightarrow$ insert 53 (insert 9 (insert 2 (insert 6 (insert 19 ($\underline{\text{sort } []}$)))))

$\Longrightarrow$ insert 53 (insert 9 (insert 2 (insert 6 ($\underline{\text{insert } 19 \, []}$))))

$\Longrightarrow$ insert 53 (insert 9 (insert 2 ($\underline{\text{insert } 6 \, [19]}$)))

$\Longrightarrow$ insert 53 (insert 9 ($\underline{\text{insert } 2 \, [6, 19]}$))

$\Longrightarrow$ insert 53 ($\underline{\text{insert } 9 \, [2, 6, 19]}$)

$\Longrightarrow$ $\underline{\text{insert } 53 \, [2, 6, 9, 19]}$

$\Longrightarrow$ $[2, 6, 9, 19, 53]$

Now we must define insert. It is a function which takes two things: the item x to be inserted and the (already-sorted) list l in which to insert it. If the list is empty, we can simply build the list $[x]$:

$$\text{insert } x \, l =$$
$$\text{if } l = [] \text{ then } [x] \text{ else} \dots$$

There are two other cases. If x is less than or equal to the head of the list, we can just put it at the front of the list, and we are done:

$$\text{insert } x \, l =$$
$$\text{if } l = [] \text{ then } [x] \text{ else}$$
$$\text{if } x \leq \text{head } l \text{ then } [x] \bullet l \text{ else} \dots$$

Otherwise, we have not yet found an appropriate place for our number, and we must keep searching. The result should be our head, followed by the insertion of our number in the tail:

$$\text{insert } x \, l =$$
$$\text{if } l = [] \text{ then } [x] \text{ else}$$
$$\text{if } x \leq \text{head } l \text{ then } [x] \bullet l \text{ else}$$
$$[\text{head } l] \bullet \text{insert } x \, (\text{tail } l)$$

Consider the evaluation of insert 3 [1, 1, 2, 3, 5, 9]:

$\underline{\text{insert } 3 \, [1, 1, 2, 3, 5, 9]}$

$\Longrightarrow$ $[1] \bullet \underline{\text{insert } 3 \, [1, 2, 3, 5, 9]}$

$\Longrightarrow$ $[1] \bullet ([1] \bullet \underline{\text{insert } 3 \, [2, 3, 5, 9]})$

$\Longrightarrow$ $[1] \bullet ([1] \bullet ([2] \bullet \underline{\text{insert } 3 \, [3, 5, 9]}))$

$\Longrightarrow$ $\underline{[1] \bullet ([1] \bullet ([2] \bullet ([3] \bullet [3, 5, 9])))}$

$\Longrightarrow$ $[1, 1, 2, 3, 3, 5, 9]$

We compare 3 with 1. Too large. We compare it with the second 1. Too large. We compare it with 2, again too large. We compare it with 3. It is equal, so we have found a place for it. The rest of the list need not be dealt with now, and the list is sorted. Here is the whole program in one place:

$$\text{insert } x \, l =$$
$$\quad \text{if } l = [] \text{ then } [x] \text{ else}$$
$$\quad \text{if } x \leq \text{head } l \text{ then } [x] \bullet l \text{ else}$$
$$\quad [\text{head } l] \bullet \text{insert } x \, (\text{tail } l)$$

$$\text{sort } l =$$
$$\quad \text{if } l = [] \text{ then } [] \text{ else insert } (\text{head } l) \, (\text{sort } (\text{tail } l))$$

In this chapter, we have covered a lot of ground, going from the most simple mathematical expressions to a complicated computer program. Doing the problems should help you to fill in the gaps.

Problems

Solutions on page 159.

1. Evaluate the following simple expressions, following normal mathematical rules and adding parentheses where needed. Show each evaluation in both tree and textual form.

   a) $1 + 1 + 1$

   b) $2 \times 2 \times 2$

   c) $2 \times 3 + 4$

2. In an environment in which $x = 4, y = 5, z = 100$, evaluate the following expressions:

   a) $x \times x \times y$

   b) $z \times y + z$

   c) $z \times z$

3. Consider the following function, which has two inputs – x and y:

$$f\, x\, y = x \times y \times x$$

   Evaluate the following expressions:

   a) f 4 5

   b) f (f 4 5) 5

   c) f (f 4 5) (f 5 4)

4. Recall the truth values *true* and *false*, and the if... then... else construction. Evaluate the following expressions:

   a) f 5 4 = f 4 5

   b) if 1 = 2 then 3 else 4

   c) if (if 1 = 2 then false else true) then 3 else 4

5. Evaluate the following list expressions:

   a) head [2,3,4]

   b) tail [2]

   c) [head [2,3,4]] • [2,3,4]

6. Consider this function, which removes elements in positions 2,4,6... from a list, leaving elements in positions 1,3,5...

$$\text{odds } l =$$
$$\text{if } l = [] \text{ then } [] \text{ else}$$
$$\text{if tail } l = [] \text{ then } l \text{ else}$$
$$[\text{head } l] \bullet \text{odds (tail (tail } x))$$

Evaluate the following uses of this function:

a) odds []

b) odds [1,2]

c) odds [1,2,3]

You need not show all the stages of evaluation, if you can do it in your head.

Chapter 8

Grey Areas

With only black ink and white paper, we can draw both beautiful letters and good line drawings, such as the diagrams of Bézier curves from Chapter 2. But what about reproducing photographs? How can we create the intermediate grey tones? Consider the following two images: a photograph of a camel and a rather higher-resolution picture of a smooth gradient between black and white:

We shall use these pictures to compare the different methods of reproduction we discuss. From looking at the page (at least if you are reading this book in physical form rather than on a computer screen), you can see that it is indeed possible, at least when one views the page from a normal reading distance. But how?

The simplest method of converting a grey image into a black and white one is simply to pick a level of grey above which we consider each part of the image black and below which we consider it white. Here is our camel, printed using black ink for any part which is more than 50% black (i.e. a mid grey), and no ink for any part which is less than 50% black:

Well, we can see the shape of the camel, but the result is less than spectacular. Let's try moving the threshold to 40%:

We can't see as much detail of the camel in this case, but at least its legs are solid. If we move the other way, to a threshold of 60%, things get even worse:

If we have to manually pick a suitable threshold for each image in a book to get even an acceptable result, the process is going to be time consuming. Here is our black to white gradient at 40%, 50%, and 60% thresholds:

These images bear almost no resemblance to the original. Before describing some more advanced methods for grey tone reproduction, like the one used to make the images at the head of this chapter, we shall take a brief historical detour – the problem of reproducing grey tones is not intrinsically one of computer printing, but has been important in newspaper and print production for hundreds of years.

The process of printing is essentially one of duplication. In former times, if we wanted just one of something, we could have a painter paint it, or a scribe write it down. We might even be able to produce a few thousand bibles by having monks copy them repeatedly for years at a time. However, we could not produce a million copies of a newspaper, with text and pictures, overnight, no matter how extensive our resources. To produce text, we require only black ink on white paper. To reproduce paintings and photographs, we need methods which provide the illusion of grey tones. Printing the paper dozens of times with diluted inks to form multiple shades of grey, as the watercolourist would, is time consuming and physically difficult – think of the amount of water which would end up on the paper, for one. So we must find other ways. The following picture shows a very simple scheme for creating an illusion of grey on a display such as a computer screen:

We have a checkerboard pattern of black and white, and if we get the scale small enough, or the viewer stands far enough away, or both, the appearance is of a mid grey. Put this book on a stand and walk slowly away – how far do you have to go for each of the parts of this picture to appear grey? Similar techniques can work when printing on paper, but we have to account for the spreading of ink and all the other imperfections of the physical world.

Some of the earliest reproduction methods involved cutting patterns into wooden blocks, applying ink, and stamping them onto cloth or paper, either by hand or in a primitive press. The process

Figure A: Woodblock print. *Der Formschnieder* (The Blockcutter), 1568.

is similar to a child cutting a potato to make a stamp – the wood is removed in areas where the artist does not want ink, and then ink is applied to the raised portions. Figure A shows a woodblock print *Der Formschnieder* (The Blockcutter) from the *Panoplia omnium illiberalium mechanicarum* (Book of Trades), published in Germany in 1568. The detail achievable depends upon the closeness of the grain of the wood, the properties of the ink and paper, and the permeability of the wood to ink. Attempts to produce areas which appear grey by using hatching or other patterns are likely to be either too coarse to be convincing, or they result in a solid inked area due to ink spreading across the surface of the block or along the fibres of the paper.

The term *intaglio* (in-<u>tah</u>-lee-o), from the Italian *intagliare* – to engrave – refers to a group of techniques in which a metal plate has material removed manually, is rubbed with viscous ink all over, has the excess removed carefully with a cloth, and is then pressed onto a dampened piece of paper. The ink remains only in the lines engraved in the plate, and is transferred to the paper by the pressure of the press. Thus, the removal of material is normally done in the opposite sense to that in the woodblock process: we engrave where we want ink to be present, not where we want it to be absent.

Figure B: Engraving. Detail of *Der Kreuzbrunnen zu Marienbad*, 1819.

The term engraving, in the context of printing, refers to the use of the tools traditionally used for engraving decoration on, for example, decorative silver-work, on metal plates instead, which are then used for printing. Decorative metal engravers had used more primitive versions of this technique to "print" their work-in-progress when designing *niello*, a type of decoration where engraved lines were filled with a black substance and polished for contrast. Making proof prints with ink helped to show what the final design might look like when blacked.

In the late fifteenth century, engraving began to be used for the reproduction of simplified versions of paintings and for original works. A copper plate would be inscribed with a hard metal tool known as a *burin*. The plate could then be used to produce hundreds of copies of a print. (Copper being soft, and the printing being done under pressure, it would eventually produce faded prints.) Engraving was a highly skilled and difficult process. Figure B is a relatively simple and coarse engraving, a detail of *Der Kreuzbrunnen zu Marienbad* published by Franz Satori in 1819. Figure C is a much more accomplished and fine engraving, *Melancolia I*, by the German master Albrecht Dürer.

Alternative intaglio methods were developed, hoping to improve the fineness of the result, or lessen the amount of expertise required. The *mezzotint* method, from the Italian "mezzo tinto"

Figure C: Fine engraving. *Melacolia I*, Albrecht Dürer, 1514.

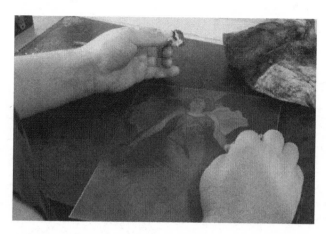

Figure D: Wiping excess ink from a mezzotint plate.

meaning "half-painted", involves using a device called a rocker to roughen the plate all over. Ink gathers in the little indentations made by such a process, leading to an entirely black image. Burnishing tools are then used to flatten the copper in areas where ink is not wanted. Because this process is gradual (one may burnish more or less), the illusion of shades is easier to achieve. Figure D shows a mezzotint plate being wiped off ready for printing. Unfortunately, due to the softness of copper and the smallness of the indentations, these plates did not last long, and the quality of the printing declined with each pressing. Figure E shows a mezzotint print. Note the fineness of the grey tone reproduction.

Another alternative to engraving is the process of *etching*, in which the whole plate is covered in an acid-resistant substance, which is then scratched off using tools in areas where the artist wants ink to appear in the final print. The plate is then washed with acid, which roughens the metal in unprotected areas so that they will hold ink. The plate is then printed as with any other intaglio process. The great advantage is that the process is available to the general artist, who can draw in this medium without learning the difficult metalwork skills of the engraver. Improvements to the process include "stopping out", where the plate is briefly dipped in the acid, more acid-resistant substance is added to certain areas, and then the plate is dipped again. This allows better control over grey tones. Figure F is an etching by Rembrandt, known as *The Hundred Guilder Print* after the sum reportedly once paid for a copy.

Figure E: A mezzotint print depicting Bertel Thorvaldsen (1770-1844), produced by Gustav Luederitz from an original by Franz Kruger.

Figure F: Etching. *Christ Headling the Sick*, or *The Hundred Guilder Print*, c. 1647–1649, Rembrandt van Rijn.

It might surprise you that even the photographic process has trouble representing grey tones. Photographic film consists of particles of compounds of silver, suspended in a gel. When exposed to light, tiny changes to the crystal structure record an invisible image. When developed, each particle is either converted to silver (which will appear black in the final photograph), or not thus converted (which will appear white). The process of enlarging the photograph from the negative to the positive paper print may introduce greys by dint of its analogue nature, of course, but if enlarged enough, one can see the so-called film grain clearly. Figure G shows an enlargement of a photograph of a plain grey card. Under a powerful electron microscope, in Figure H, we can see the individual crystals on the photographic film. None of the methods we have seen so far allow for the automatic conversion of photographic content to a printable form such as a plate which might be wanted for a daily newspaper. We have a grey tone image, in the form of a photographic negative. Our printing process, however, allows only black and white, so we wish to automatically convert the grey tones to a series of regularly spaced dots whose diameter reflects the level of grey. Here is our gradient, followed by its so-called *halftone*:

Figure G: Film grain

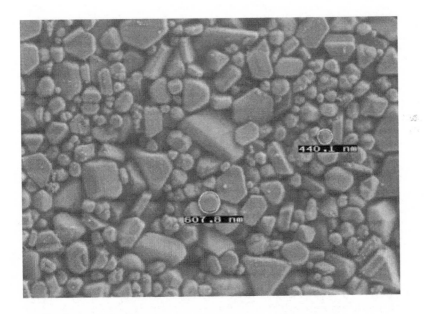

Figure H: Film under an electron microscope.

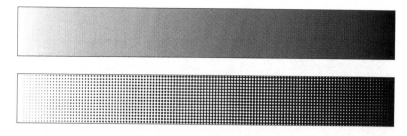

You can see that the spacing of the dots is quite wide, and that they can be quite large: this is counterintuitive but deliberate. By making sure that the dots are properly separate, we make the image easily reproducible, even on cheap, porous newsprint. Perhaps 50 to 80 lines of dots per inch is sufficient. For higher-quality coated paper used in book production, we might be able to go as far as 150 lines per inch or lpi.

Early methods of halftone production involved placing a device known as a halftone screen in front of photographic paper and projecting the original image through it with the use of a camera lens. The first halftone screens were made in about 1850 from a fine cloth gauze by the British scientist William Henry Fox Talbot (1800–1877). Later, they were commercially manufactured from glass engraved with a grid of lines. The effect of these is, through optical effects, to project a halftone image – a series of distinct dots of varying size – onto the photographic paper. This can then be used as the starting point for producing plates for printing. The image has successfully been reduced to only black and white through purely physical means. Figure I is one of the earliest halftoned pictures in mass production: it shows Steinway Hall on East 14th Street in Manhattan, printed in the Daily Graphic on December 2nd 1873. This was the first method of printing a photograph direct from the negative with no manual intervention.

Returning to Computer Science, we can simulate the halftone screen in software, to produce the appropriate dot pattern for printing. Consider the three versions of our camel picture in Figure J. The first one, with the smallest dots, seems to have the highest effective sharpness and visual resolution. However, as the maximum dot size increases, so does the number of possible shades. The middle image, when viewed at a distance, is in fact a closer representation of the original image. The last one has yet more sizes of dots (and so, effective grey levels) but the resolution is now too coarse. We turn to our gradient for another look, printed in the same halftones as the camel pictures:

Figure I: Halftone of the Steinway Hall, printed in the Daily Graphic, December 2nd 1873.

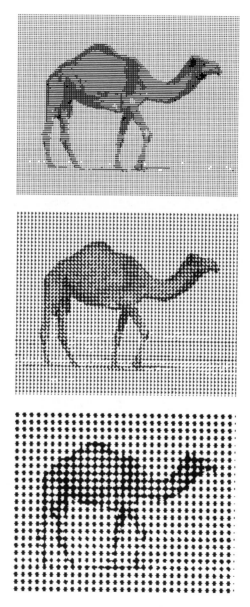

Figure J: Small, medium, and large halftone dots.

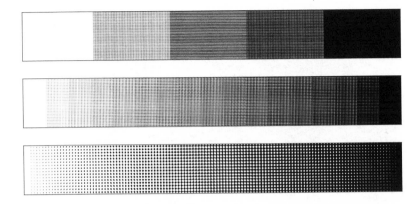

At the top, the finest halftone; at the bottom, the coarsest. We can see that the larger number of apparent greys in the coarser dots are an advantage in this case: the top line looks very fragmented indeed. At a distance, the middle and bottom are both good.

We can perform this halftoning by producing patterns which look like increasing sizes of ink dots. These patterns can then be displayed on screen or printed. To do this, we divide the image up into little 2x2 or 4x4 squares of pixels, and then choose one of a set of patterns to represent the average level of grey in the square. The result is a picture with the same number of pixels, but where each is black or white. Here are the patterns for a 2x2 scheme:

Notice that there are five patterns, not four as we might expect. We use the first pattern for a grey level between 0% and 20%, the second between 20% and 40%, and so forth. In this scheme we have tried to keep the black dots adjacent to one another to build up little spots, which is better suited to the spreading behaviour of ink on paper. The process is known as *dithering*. The patterns above may be generated by listing the order in which they turn black in a table:

$$1 \quad 2$$
$$3 \quad 4$$

So, for the third pattern, we blacken all pixels with values less than three (that is, one and two). It is known as an *ordered dither* for this reason. Here is the result:

We only have five different shades of grey, and the image suffers for it: we can see areas which in the original image were subtly shaded as plain, flat sections – not a good result. Let's double the length of the side of our square to 4. Now, we will have $4 \times 4 + 1 =$ 17 different levels of grey, but the image will have fewer dots overall. Will the increase in the number of shades outweigh the decrease in apparent resolution? Here is the generating table:

$$
\begin{array}{cccc}
15 & 10 & 8 & 14 \\
4 & 1 & 2 & 12 \\
11 & 3 & 4 & 6 \\
13 & 7 & 9 & 16
\end{array}
$$

Here are the resultant 17 dither patterns. Again, they form a cohesive spot, and are built up somewhat symmetrically:

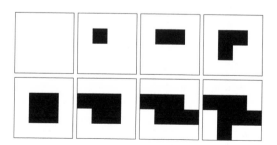

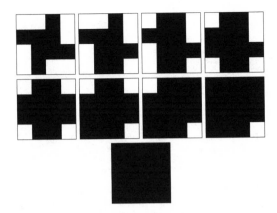

As the tone moves from white to black, the spot grows gradually. If you imagine the patterns tiled repeatedly across the page, you can see that the white sections left in the corners as the black spot grows themselves form white spots. Thus, we have a smooth transition. Here is the result of dithering with these patterns for the camel and the gradient:

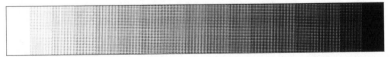

Prop this book up against a wall, retreat to the other side of the room (or perhaps half-way), and see which looks more camel-like. What about at normal reading distance? Such halftone patterns are used in most modern printing. Here are microscope pictures of the camel as it is printed at the head of this chapter, at 20x and 400x magnification:

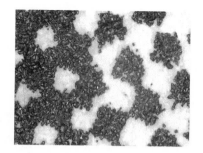

For colour images, several halftone screens are used, one for each of the primary printing colours used in the particular printing technology – often cyan, magenta, yellow, and black. The halftones are at different angles, so that the colours do not interfere with one another and the ink is more evenly distributed. Here is part of a glossy colour leaflet at 20x and 400x:

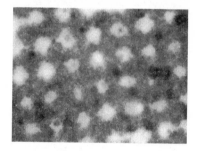

When we are producing a result for a type of device which has reasonably sharp or predictable dots (such as a computer monitor) and none of the vagaries of ink-flow, we can choose a more appropriate ordered dither, free of the need to build a spot as such, leading to the appearance of a higher resolution. Black and white computer displays are rather rare these days, but were common in the past. Consider the following table and pattern for the 2x2 case:

2   3
4   1

We still have five levels of grey, but the apparent resolution should be higher, and the eye should find it harder to discern individual dots, since we try to keep them as small as possible for as long as possible. Here is the camel and gradient, drawn with this new set of patterns:

Here is a similarly-constructed 4x4 pattern giving, as before, 17 greys. Notice that it is built in such a way as to keep the spots as small as possible.

2	16	3	13
10	6	11	7
4	14	1	15
12	8	9	5

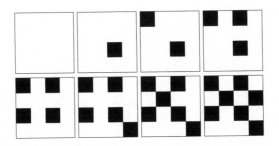

This time, the results are rather better, due to the increased number of dot patterns, which allow a wider range of apparent shades of grey to be reproduced. Here is our camel and gradient built with the 4x4 patterns generated from our table:

The spots are, in general, much smaller than in the first set of patterns we looked at, and the gradient is reasonably convincing, although it does appear to be divided into little blocks. Figure K shows our camel picture using these sorts of small-dot dither patterns of sizes 2x2, 4x4, and 8x8. The difference is even more obvious when we use the gradient:

Figure K: Small-spot ordered dithers with 2x2, 4x4, and 8x8 patterns.

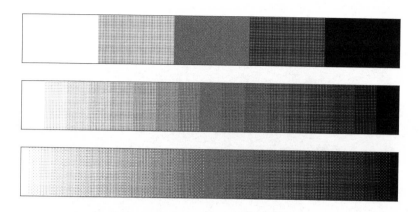

Our small-dot ordered dither patterns, suitable for on-screen use where pixels are clearly defined (unlike ink on paper), are not too bad. They do the job of creating the impression of grey shades where only black and white exist. However, the regular patterns of dots can be distracting: we see those patterns instead of the image, since our eyes are drawn to regular features. The technique of *error diffusion* leads to a better result than ordered dithering, with fewer distracting patterns. This method was invented in 1976 by Robert W. Floyd and his student Louis Steinberg at Stanford University. Say that we have an image made up of greys numbered between 0% ink (white) and 100% ink (black) like the one in this diagram – unavoidably, we shall have to use a somewhat small example:

$$
\begin{array}{ccc}
50 & 20 & 70 \\
40 & 30 & 70 \\
50 & 40 & 90
\end{array}
$$

We proceed pixel by pixel, starting at the top left, dealing with a row of pixels in order and then moving on to the next row, until we have looked at the whole image. For each pixel, we first decide whether to paint it black or white in the final image. If it is 50 percent or more black, we make that pixel black; if it is less than 50 percent, we make it white. We write this value to the final image. Now we consider the error inherent in that choice – that is to say, how much too white or too black were we forced to make the pixel due to only having fully white and fully black available. For example, on the first pixel, we would choose to place a 100% black pixel, and the original value was 50%, so we were forced to make it 50% too black. We redistribute this error to some of the surrounding pixels of the original image according to the following proportions (where × marks the current pixel):

$$\times \qquad 7/16$$
$$3/16 \quad 5/16 \quad 1/16$$

So, for our first pixel, the error of -50% is distributed among the surrounding ones in the following amounts:

$$\times \qquad -22\%$$
$$-9\% \quad -16\% \quad -3\%$$

We apply this arithmetic to the original image to obtain the following values:

$$\begin{array}{ccc} 100 & -2 & 70 \\ 31 & 14 & 67 \\ 50 & 40 & 90 \end{array}$$

Now we can move on to the next pixel. And so on, all across the first row, and onto the next, until the image is wholly dealt with. The end result should be that the final image only has the values 0 and 100, so it has been successfully reduced to just black and white. The overall average grey level of the image should be the same, because the errors have been only moved around, not forgotten about (except at the edge of the image, where the errors "fall off"). Here is the end result for our image:

$$\begin{array}{ccc} 100 & 0 & 100 \\ 0 & 0 & 100 \\ 100 & 0 & 100 \end{array}$$

A useful feature of this scheme is that a flat mid grey at fifty percent will produce a stable, miniature checkerboard pattern, which is not distracting since it is so small. Consider the following original:

$$\begin{array}{ccc} 50 & 50 & 50 \\ 50 & 50 & 50 \\ 50 & 50 & 50 \end{array}$$

The final image, after each pixel has been processed, will have the following pattern of black and white pixels:

100   0   100

0   100   0

100   0   100

Here is our camel picture and gradient processed with the algorithm described above.

You can see that there appear to be much finer gradations of grey and that, whilst the eye can discern some patterns in the flat shaded areas, they are much less distracting than in the case of the ordered dither. Overall, a much more pleasing result. The gradient is much finer too, especially when viewed from a distance. There are several newer variations on this procedure, using more complicated diffusion of errors.

Problems

Solutions on page 163.

Show the 17 dither patterns generated from each of these grids of numbers.

1.	1	9	3	11
	13	5	15	7
	4	12	2	10
	16	8	14	6

2.	1	9	13	3
	16	5	7	11
	12	8	6	15
	4	14	10	2

3.	2	6	11	15
	4	8	9	13
	14	10	7	3
	16	12	5	1

Chapter 9

Our Typeface

This book is typeset in Palatino, designed in 1950 by the legendary German typographer Hermann Zapf (1918–2015). The definitive modern version of Palatino from Linotype of Germany contains some 1328 *glyphs* (shapes for characters) for each typeface in the family (Roman [normal], *Italic*, **Bold**, and ***Bold Italic***), a total of 5312 shapes for the typeface designer to draw. You can see why commissioning a new typeface is expensive, and so why buying high quality typefaces for your own use can be expensive too. Due to all the extra characters available, Palatino Linotype supports the following Western languages by providing appropriate accents and alternative glyphs in a single typeface:

Afrikaans	Estonian	Latvian	Serbian
Albanian	Faroese	Lithuanian	Slovak
Basque	Finnish	Macedonian	Slovenian
Belarusian	French	Malay	Somali
Bulgarian	Galician	Maltese	Spanish
Catalan	German	Manx	Swahili
Cornish	Hungarian	Norwegian Bokmål	Swedish
Croatian	Icelandic	Norwegian Nynorsk	Swiss German
Czech	Indonesian	Oromo	Uzbek
Danish	Irish	Polish	Vietnamese
Dutch	Italian	Portuguese	Welsh
English	Kalaallisut	Romanian	Zulu
Esperanto	Kazakh	Russian	

In addition, it contains the Cyrillic characters used in Modern Greek as well as the so-called Latin ones we use in English. Here are the capital letters and lower-case letters used in English.

A B C D E F G H I J K
L M N O P Q R S T U
V W X Y Z

a b c d e f g h i j k
l m n o p q r s t u
v w x y z

Then, two styles of numbers: the so-called *lining numbers*, which have the same height as capital letters, and all sit on the baseline, and the *old style numbers*, some of which have descenders, and are not all the height of capital letters.

0123456789

0123456789

Below are some of the *ligatures* available in Palatino. These are special glyphs used when letters would otherwise join unpleasantly, or in other situations where two letters should be represented by a single glyph. Some are for decoration (such as "Q" followed by "u", which is normally just Qu). Others look like ligatures, but are really a different sound or letter, a diphthong, such as œ.

IJ Qu Th æœ
fi fl ff ffi ffl fk ffk fj
sþ st tt tz ch ck ct

Next are the Small Caps, which are capital letters set to the same height as lowercase letters. You can see examples of Small Caps in the front matter of this book (the parts before the first chapter). Notice that the small caps are not just scaled-down versions of the ordinary capitals – having the same general weight, they may be used alongside them.

SMALL CAPS

Next, we have accented letters, of which only a tiny portion are shown here. Accents attach in different places on each letter, so many typefaces contain an accented version of each common letter-accent pair, together with separate accent marks which can be combined with other letters as required for more esoteric uses.

Ä À Å Á Ã Ą Â Ç
ä à å á ã ą â ç

Finally, here are some of the many other glyphs in Palatino, for currency symbols and so forth, and some of the punctuation:

@ £ $ % ¶ † ‡ © ¥ €

` ı ` ` ` ` ` ` `

! ? ( ) { } : ; , . /

How do we pick letters from the typeface and place them on
the page? Each glyph contains not only the lines and curves we
have discussed earlier in the books, but what are known as *metrics*;
that is to say a set of numbers governing how the letter relates to
its previous ones horizontally, and where it lies vertically. Various
of these numbers can be used to fit letters together pleasingly. The
most important metrics are the *baseline* and the *advancement*. The
baseline is just like the line on a schoolchild's ruled paper – capital
letters sit on it, letters with descenders like "g" and "y" drop somewhat below it. Every glyph is defined in relation to this baseline, so
we can place it in the correct vertical position. The advancement
tells us how much to move to the right after drawing the glyph;
that is to say, how far the origin has moved. So, at the beginning of
a line, we start at an x-coordinate of zero and move rightwards by
the advancement each time.

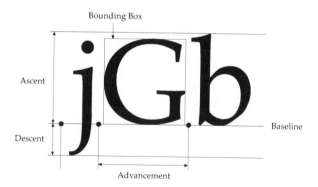

The diagram shows three glyphs, showing various metrics:
some are needed for placing them on the page and some information used for other purposes. The position of the letters in a line
depends not only on the individual characters (the letter "i" is much
narrower than the letter "w", for example), but on the combinations
in which they are printed. For example, a capital V followed by a
capital A looks odd if the spacing is not tightened:

AV AV

In this example, there is no tightening in the left-hand example, but tightening has been applied to the right-hand one. Such tightening is called *kerning*. Here are some of the rules from Palatino showing how much extra space is added or removed when the characters "A", "a", ":" etc. follow the character "V".

V A -111	V hyphen -74	V r -92
V a -92	V i -55	V semicolon -55
V colon -55	V o -111	V u -92
V comma -129	V period -129	V y -92
V e -111	V A -111	V Oslash -37
V OE -37	V ae -148	V oslash -130
V oe -130	V Aring -130	V quoteright 28

The numbers are expressed in thousandths of an inch. For example, you can see that when a hyphen follows a "V", the hyphen is placed 74/1000 of an inch closer to the "V". Kerning is especially important when letters meet punctuation. Palatino had, in all, 1031 such rules for pairs of characters. Overlapping of adjacent letters can also be achieved simply by extending the shape of the character beyond its bounding box. The following diagram shows the particularly striking overlaps used by the various alternative characters available in another of Zapf's creations, the script-like Zapfino.

dawning dawning dawning dawning

dawning dawning dawning dawning

The diagram shows various alternative characters for "d" and "g" in the Zapfino typeface. You can see that some suit the word more than others. In particular, in the bottom-right example, the initial "d" clashes awfully with the next letter.

Before computers, when type was set manually using little metal pieces arranged into rows, smeared in ink, and pressed onto paper, it was natural for a typeface to have slightly different glyph designs for each size. A headline would have a subtly different character design to normal sized text, and again different to the sort of tiny text used for footnotes. Part of this is due to the essential optical characteristics of small shapes: it is easier to read a small typeface if it has proportionally wider characters than its normal size, for example. Part of it has to do with the physical characteristics of the ink and paper: ink spreads, and the way it spreads leads to the same metal shape showing differently at different sizes.

When designing a typeface by computer, however, it is tempting to take a shortcut: design the typeface once, and then automatically scale it to whatever size is needed by simple arithmetic on its coordinates. Now, we have any size available, and designing the typeface is cheaper. This shortcut was not available to the metal type manufacturer. However, many good modern computer typefaces still have multiple so-called *optical sizes*. They may have separate shapes for 5pt, 8pt, 10pt, 12pt, and 16pt, for example. We can use the computer scaling method in between sizes – to obtain 11pt, for example. Figure A on the opposite page shows a phrase printed in the Latin Modern typeface, at five different sizes. Below, the same phrase has been repeated, but scaled up to show the differences clearly. We have not yet looked at the other three faces of the Palatino typeface: the **Bold**, the *Italic*, and the ***Bold Italic***. A bold typeface is one which is thicker, using more ink. The Italic has a different, sloping shape. Both are used for emphasis. You can see Bold and Italic used in various places in this book, but we don't use Bold Italic. The various shapes are designed to work comfortably together.

Shape **Shape**

Shape ***Shape***

Optical Font Sizes
Optical Font Sizes
Optical Font Sizes
Optical Font Sizes
Optical Font Sizes

Optical Font Sizes
Optical Font Sizes
Optical Font Sizes
Optical Font Sizes
Optical Font Sizes

Figure A

You can see that the Italic has an entirely different shape from the Roman. This is usual for *serif* typefaces such as Palatino. (Serifs are the little pieces attached to the end of each stroke of the letter.) However, for a sans serif typeface (one without serifs), it is sufficient to simply slant the shapes by fifteen degrees or so. This can be done automatically by the computer, so the typeface designer need only design the Roman shapes. Unfortunately, automatically producing a Bold face from a Roman one is rather more difficult, so it is usually done manually, albeit with help from computer tools. This diagram shows an automatically-generated oblique face and a separately-designed italic face:

Oblique Italic

Oblique Italic

We have looked at some of the surprising complexities of a simple typeface, and how its characters are picked and placed next to each other to form lines. Typefaces for Eastern alphabets and writing systems are even more complex. To finish, we exhibit the full 1328 glyphs of the Palatino Roman typeface on the next three pages. Can you work out what each glyph is used for?

@ A B C D E F G H I J K L M N O
P Q R S T U V W X Y Z Á À Â Ä Ã Ă Å
Ǻ Ā Ą Æ Ǽ Ć Ĉ Č Ç Ċ Ď Ð Đ É È Ê Ë Ě
Ĕ Ė Ē Ę Ǵ Ĝ Ğ Ģ Ġ Ĥ Ħ Í Ì Î Ï Ĩ Ĭ Į
Ī Į Ĵ Ķ Ķ Ĺ Ļ Ľ Ļ Ł Ł Ń Ñ Ň Ņ Ņ Ó Ò
Ô Ö Õ Ȯ Ő Ō Ø Ǿ Œ Ŕ Ř Ŗ Ŗ Ś Ŝ Š Ş Ş
Ţ Ť Ť Ţ Ŧ Ú Ù Û Ü Ũ Ŭ Ů Ű Ū Ų Ẃ Ẁ Ŵ
Ẅ Ý Ỳ Ŷ Ÿ Ź Ž Ż 3 Ŋ ŋ Þ a b c d e f
g h i j k l m n o p q r s t u v w x
y z á à â ä ã ă å ǻ ā ą æ ǽ ć ĉ č ç
ċ ď đ é è ê ë ě ĕ ė ē ę ǵ ĝ ğ ġ ġ ĥ
ħ í ì î ï ĩ ĭ ı ī į ĵ ķ ķ ĸ ĺ ļ ľ ļ
ł ł ń ñ ň ņ ʼn ņ ó ò ô ö õ ŏ ő ō ø ǿ
œ ŕ ř ŗ ŗ ś ŝ š ş ş ţ ť ţ ŧ ú ù û ü
ũ ŭ ů ű ū ų ẃ ẁ ŵ ẅ ý ỳ ŷ ÿ ź ž ż ʒ
ŋ þ ð ß SS IJ Qu Th ch ck ct fi fl ff ffi ffl ft fft
fb ffb fh ffh fk ffk fj ij ſ ſi ſl ſſ ſſi ſſl ſt ſb ſh ſk
ſp ſt tt tz ᵃ ᵒ ⁿ a b c d e f g h i j k
l m n o p q r s t u v w x y z æ œ è
0 1 2 3 4 5 6 7 8 9 0 1 2 3 4 5 6 7
8 9 0 1 2 3 4 5 6 7 8 9 0 1 2 3 4 5
6 7 8 9 0 1 2 3 4 5 6 7 8 9 + − = (
) + − = ( ) · , $ ¢ % ‰ ¹/ ½ ⅓ ⅔ ¼ ¾
⅕ ⅖ ⅗ ⅘ ⅙ ⅚ ⅛ ⅜ ⅝ ⅞ $\frac{1}{1}$ $\frac{1}{2}$ $\frac{1}{3}$ $\frac{2}{3}$ $\frac{1}{4}$ $\frac{3}{4}$ $\frac{1}{5}$ $\frac{2}{5}$
$\frac{3}{5}$ $\frac{4}{5}$ $\frac{1}{6}$ $\frac{5}{6}$ $\frac{1}{8}$ $\frac{3}{8}$ $\frac{5}{8}$ $\frac{7}{8}$ + ± − ÷ × = ≠ ≈ < >

Palatino, glyphs 1–500

≤ ≥ ^ ~ √ ‾ ∞ ∂ Δ ∏ Σ Ω F ∫ ◊ ¬ ⌐ ≡
≅ ∪ ∩ ∨ ∧ ¤ ° # ¥ ¥ $ $ $ £ £ ¢ ƒ ₡
Œ € £ ₱ ₧ ₨ F & „ . , : ; … .. ? ¿ !
¡ ‼ ? ( ) [ ] { } ' ' " " ‚ ` ' " .
• ‹ › « » – — ¶ ¶ @ % † ‡ § * ℮ © ®
ᵀᴹ ′ ″ ℓ □ ▪ ▫ ● ○ OBJ / \ ∕ | ‖ ¦ - –
— —   ´ ` ^ ..
~ ˇ ˘ ˚   . ″ ¯ ‚ ´ ` ^ .. ~ ˇ ˘
˚   . ˏ ˏ   ´ ` ^ .. ~ ˘ ˘ ˚   .
˝ ˎ ˗ ˏ А Ă Б В Г Ѓ Ғ Д Е Ё È Ĕ Ж Җ Ӂ
З Ҙ И Й Ӣ Ѝ К Ќ Қ Ҟ Ҡ Л М Н Ң О П Р
С Ҫ Т У Ұ Ў Ў Ӯ Ӳ Ф Х Ҳ Ц Ч Ҷ Ҹ Ш Щ
Ъ Ы Ь Э Ә Ю Я Ћ Җ Ө Ѳ Ѵ Г Ï Ї Ј Ѕ Є
һ Ћ Ђ Џ Љ Њ а ă б в г ѓ ғ д е ё è ĕ
ж җ ӂ ◎ ◎ ◎ з ҙ и й ӣ ѝ к ќ қ ҟ ҡ л
м н ң о п р с ҫ т у ў ұ ҳ ӯ ӳ ф х х
ц ч ҷ ҹ ш щ ъ ы ь э ә ю я ђ є ѕ і ї
ј љ њ һ ћ џ ѣ ѣ җ ө ѳ ѵ г № ˜ ˘ Α Β
Γ Δ Ε Ζ Η Θ Ι Κ Λ Μ Ν Ξ Ο Π Ρ Σ Τ Υ
Φ Χ Ψ Ω Ἀ Ἁ Ἂ Ἃ Ἄ Ἅ Ἆ Ἇ Ά ᾼ ᾊ ᾋ ᾌ ᾍ
ᾎ ᾏ ᾈ Ᾰ Ᾱ Ὰ Ά ᾼ Ἐ Ἑ Ἒ Ἓ Ἔ Ἕ Ὲ Έ Η
Ἠ Ἡ Ἢ Ἣ Ἤ Ἥ Ἦ Ἧ Ή ᾘ ᾙ ᾚ ᾛ ᾜ ᾝ ᾞ ᾟ Ὴ Ή
ᾞ Ἰ Ἱ Ἲ Ἳ Ἴ Ἵ Ἶ Ἷ Ί Ὶ Ί Ῐ Ῑ Ῐ Ῑ Ὀ Ὁ Ὂ
Ὃ Ὄ Ὅ Ὸ Ό Ο Ρ Ῥ Ὺ Ύ Ὑ Ὓ Ὕ Ὗ Ύ Ὺ Ύ Ω
Ὠ Ὡ Ὢ Ὣ Ὤ Ὥ Ὦ Ὧ ᾨ ᾩ ᾪ ᾫ ᾬ ᾭ ᾮ ᾯ Ω Ώ

Palatino, glyphs 501–1000. (The blank ones are spaces of various widths and types.)

Ω ι α β γ δ ε ζ η θ ι κ λ μ ν ξ ο π ϱ
ς σ τ υ φ χ ψ ω ϐ ϑ ϕ ϖ ἀ ά ὰ ᾄ ᾀ ἄ
ᾶ ἆ ᾆ ᾰ ᾱ ᾳ ᾴ ᾲ ᾷ ᾂ ᾅ ᾃ ᾇ ᾰ ᾱ ᾀ ᾳ ᾴ
ᾶ ᾲ ἐ έ ὲ ἔ ἒ ἕ ἓ ἕ ἓ ή ή ὴ ᾔ ᾕ ᾗ ᾖ
ῆ ῂ ῄ ᾔ ᾕ ᾖ ᾗ ᾓ ᾒ ᾕ ᾗ ᾓ ῂ η ή ῆ ῇ ἰ
ἳ ἱ ἲ ἵ ἴ ἷ ἶ ἵ ἴ ῑ ῒ ῗ ῐ ῑ ῒ ῐ ῑ ῗ
ὁ ό ὸ ὄ ὂ ὅ ὃ ὅ ὃ ϱ ϱ ϋ ϋ ὑ ὕ ὓ ὕ ὓ
ὕ ὗ ὕ ὓ ῡ ὗ ὗ ὕ ὕ ὗ ῡ ῡ ὣ ώ ὼ ᾤ ᾠ ὥ
ᾦ ᾧ ᾢ ᾥ ᾣ ᾡ ᾤ ᾠ ᾥ ᾣ ᾦ ᾧ ᾣ ᾢ ᾡ ω ώ ῶ
ϛ ϛ ℔ ϰ ; ʼ ʹ ˙ ̈ · ̃ ̓ ̔
ʹ ˎ ʽ ˜ ˏ ˕ ˌ ‥ ‧ ˘ ˉ   Ơ ơ Ư ư đ .
ˋ ˊ ˜ ˀ   A B C D E F G H I J K L M N
O P Q R S T U V W X Y Z Á À Â Ä Ã Ă
Å Ő Ā Ą Æ Ǽ Ć Ĉ Č Ç Ċ Ď Đ Đ É È Ê Ë
Ě Ĕ Ė Ē Ę Ǵ Ĝ Ğ Ģ Ġ Ĥ Ħ Í Ì Î Ï Ĩ Ĭ
İ Ī Į Ĵ Ķ Ķ Ĺ Ļ Ľ Ļ Ŀ Ł Ń Ñ Ň Ņ Ņ Ó
Ò Ô Ö Õ Ŏ Ő Ō Ø Ǿ Œ Ŕ Ř Ŗ Ŗ Ś Ŝ Š Ş
Ş Ţ Ť Ť Ţ Ŧ Ú Ù Û Ü Ũ Ŭ Ů Ű Ū Ų Ẃ Ẁ
Ŵ Ẅ Ý Ỳ Ŷ Ÿ Ź Ž Ż Þ Ĳ ¿ ¡ & Ą ą Å
å Ấ ấ Ầ ầ Ẩ ẩ Ẫ ẫ Ậ ậ Ắ ắ Ằ ằ Ẳ ẳ Ẵ
ẵ Ặ ặ Ę ę Ế ế Ẽ ẽ Ế ế Ề ề Ể ể Ễ ễ Ệ
ệ Ỉ ỉ Ị ị Ọ ọ Ó ó Ố ố Ồ ồ Ổ ổ Ỗ õ Ộ
ộ Ớ ớ Ờ ờ Ở ở Õ õ Ợ ợ Ụ ụ Ủ ủ Ứ ứ Ừ
ừ Ử ử Ữ ữ Ự ự Ỵ ỵ Ỷ ỷ Ỹ ỹ Ǽ

Palatino, glyphs 1000–1328

Problems

Solutions on page 166.

The following words have been badly spaced. Photocopy or print out this page, cut out the letters, and then paste them onto another page along a straight line, finding an arrangement which is neither too tight nor too loose.

1. **Palatino**

2. AVER SION

3. *Conjecture*

Chapter 10

Words to Paragraphs

We have learned how to design individual characters of a typeface using lines and curves, and how to combine them into lines. Now we must combine the lines into paragraphs, and the paragraphs into pages. Look at the following two paragraphs from Franz Kafka's *Metamorphosis*:

> One morning, when Gregor Samsa woke from troubled dreams, he found himself transformed in his bed into a horrible vermin. He lay on his armour-like back, and if he lifted his head a little he could see his brown belly, slightly domed and divided by arches into stiff sections. The bedding was hardly able to cover it and seemed ready to slide off any moment. His many legs, pitifully thin compared with the size of the rest of him, waved about helplessly as he looked.
>
> "What's happened to me?" he thought. It wasn't a dream. His room, a proper human room although a little too small, lay peacefully between its four familiar walls. A collection of textile samples lay spread out on the table – Samsa was a travelling salesman – and above it there hung a picture that he had recently cut out of an illustrated magazine and housed in a nice, gilded frame. It showed a lady fitted out with a fur hat and fur boa who sat upright, raising a heavy fur muff that covered the whole of her lower arm towards the viewer.

What do we notice? The left and right hand sides of the block of text are straight – no ragged edges. This is called *full justification*. We notice that some of the lines have a hyphen at the end, in the middle of a word. Looking carefully, we see that the spacing between words is not consistent from line to line. The last line of each paragraph does not go all the way to the end; the first may be indented.

How do we build a line from a list of letters? We know that each letter in a typeface has an origin, as well as an advancement which specifies how far to move to the right after drawing a character. We know also about kerning, which tells us that certain letter combinations must appear closer together. Here is a line of text, showing the (usually invisible) boxes which help to position each character:

"What's happened to me", he thought.

"What'shappenedtome",hethought.

If all our characters fortuitously added up to the correct width for a line, or we were happy to break words with hyphens any-where, or we did not want a straight right edge, this is all we would have to do. We would draw the characters in order until we reached the end of a line, and then start on the next line, moving down the page the right amount (called the *leading* – pronounced "ledding"). Alas, the world is not that simple, and we must add space to fill out the line. This can look poor if done badly, especially when a narrow column is used, such as in a newspaper:

F   u   l   l
justification   in
a   narrow
column   can
make   big   gaps
between   words
and letters.

Here, space has been added not only between words but be-tween letters, to make the line fit. Generally, we like to add most of the needed space between words, rather than between individ-ual letters. Here is a paragraph typeset to three different column widths:

One morning, when Gregor Samsa woke from troubled dreams, he found himself transformed in his bed into a horrible vermin. He lay on his armour-like back, and if he...

One morning, when Gregor Samsa woke from troubled dreams, he found himself transformed in his bed into a horrible vermin. He lay on his armour-like back, and if he lifted his head a little he could see his brown belly, slightly domed and divided by arches into stiff sections.

One morning, when Gregor Samsa woke from troubled dreams, he found himself transformed in his bed into a horrible vermin. He lay on his armour-like back, and if he lifted his head a little he could see his brown belly, slightly domed and divided by arches into stiff sections.

Notice how the result improves as the column becomes wider; fewer compromises have to be made. In fact, no hyphens at all were required in the widest case. In the narrowest column, we have refused to add extra space between the letters of the compound word "armour-like", but chose rather to produce an underfull line in this case. This decision is a matter of taste, of course. Another option is to give up on the idea of straight left and right edges, and set the text *ragged-right*. The idea is to make no changes in the spacing of words at all, just ending a line when the next word will not fit. This also eliminates hyphenation. Here is a paragraph set first ragged right, and then fully justified:

One morning, when Gregor Samsa woke from troubled dreams, he found himself transformed in his bed into a horrible vermin. He lay on his armour-like back, and if he lifted his head a little he could see his brown belly, slightly domed and divided by arches into stiff sections.

One morning, when Gregor Samsa woke from troubled dreams, he found himself transformed in his bed into a horrible vermin. He lay on his armour-like back, and if he lifted his head a little he could see his brown belly, slightly domed and divided by arches into stiff sections.

If we decide we must hyphenate a word because we cannot stretch or shrink a line without making it too ugly, how do we choose where to break it? We could just hyphenate as soon as the line is full, irrespective of where we are in the word. In the following example, the paragraph on the left prefers hyphenation at any point to adding or removing space between words. The paragraph on the right follows usual typesetting and hyphenation rules, preferring the adding of space to hyphenation.

One morning, when Gregor Samsa woke from trouble-d dreams, he found hims-elf transformed in his bed into a horrible vermin. He lay on his armour-like back, and if he lifted his head a little he could see his brow-n belly, slightly domed and divided by arches into stiff sections.	One morning, when Gregor Samsa woke from trou-bled dreams, he found himself transformed in his bed into a horrible vermin. He lay on his armour-like back, and if he lifted his head a little he could see his brown belly, slightly domed and divided by arches into stiff sections.

These are very ugly hyphenations, however: we have "trouble-d", "hims-elf", and "brow-n". Every word has places which are better or worse for hyphenation. We would prefer "trou-bled" and "him-self". Ideally "brown" should not be hyphenated at all. Some words must be hyphenated differently depending on context: "rec-ord" for the noun, "re-cord" for the verb, for example. In addition, authorities on hyphenation (such as dictionaries which include hyphenation information) do not always agree: Webster has "in-de-pen-dent" and "tri-bune", American Heritage has "in-de-pend-ent" and "trib-une". There are words which should never be hyphenated. For example, there is no really good place to break "squirm".

There are two methods for solving this problem automatically as the computer typesets the lines: a *dictionary-based* system simply stores an entire word list with the hyphenation points for each word. This ensures perfect hyphenation for known words, but does not help us at all when a new word is encountered (as it often is in scientific or technical publications, or if we need to hyphenate a proper noun, such as a the name of a person or city). The alternative is a *rule-based* system, which follows a set of rules about what are typically good and bad breaks. For example "a break is always allowable after "q" if followed by a vowel" or "a hyphen is fine before -ness" or "a hyphen is good between "x" and "p" in all circumstances". We may also have *inhibiting* rules such as "never break b-ly". Some patterns may only apply at the beginning or end of a word, others apply anywhere. In fact, these rules can be derived automatically from a list of the correct hyphenations, and be expected to work well for other unknown words (assuming those words are in the same language – we require a hyphenation dictionary for each language appearing in the document). For example, in the typesetting system used for this book, there are 8527 rules, and only 8 exceptional cases which must be listed explicitly:

```
uni-ver-sity      ma-nu-scripts
uni-ver-sit-ies   re-ci-pro-city
how-ever          through-out
ma-nu-script      some-thing
```

Thus far, we have assumed that decisions on hyphenation are made once we reach the end of a line and find we are about to overrun it. If we are, we alter the spacing between words, or hyphenate, or some combination of the two. And so, at most we need to re-typeset the current line. Advanced line breaking algorithms use a more complicated approach, seeking to optimise the result for a whole paragraph. (We have gone line-by-line, making the best line we can for the first line, then the second etc.) It may turn out that an awkward situation later in the paragraph is prevented by making a slightly less-than-optimal decision in an earlier line, such as squeezing in an extra word or hyphenating in a good position when not strictly required. We can assign "demerits" to certain situations (a hyphenation, too much or too little spacing between words, and so on) and optimise the outcome for the least sum of such demerits. These sorts of optimisation algorithms can be quite slow for large paragraphs, taking an amount of time equal to the square of the number of lines in the paragraph. For normal texts, this is not a problem, since we are unlikely to have more than a few tens of lines in a single paragraph.

We have now dealt with splitting a text into lines and paragraphs, but similar problems occur when it comes to fitting those paragraphs onto a page. There are two worrying situations: when the last line of a paragraph is "widowed" at the top of the next page, and when the first line of a paragraph is "orphaned" on the last line of a page. Examples of a widow and an orphan are shown on the next page. It is difficult to deal with these problems without upsetting the balance of the whole two-page spread, but it can be done by slightly increasing or decreasing line spacing on one side. Another option, of course, is to edit the text, and you may be surprised to learn how often that happens.

Further small adjustments and improvements to reduce the amount of hyphenation can be introduced using so-called *microty-pography*. This involves stretching or shrinking the individual char-

quis tortor vitae risus porta vehicula.

Fusce mauris. Vestibulum luctus nibh at lectus. Sed bibendum, nulla a faucibus semper, leo velit ultricies tellus, ac venenatis arcu wisi vel nisl. Vestibulum diam. Aliquam pellentesque, augue quis sagittis posuere, turpis lacus congue quam, in hendrerit risus eros eget felis. Maecenas eget erat in sapien mattis porttitor. Vestibulum porttitor. Nulla facilisi. Sed a turpis eu lacus commodo facilisis. Morbi fringilla, wisi in dignissim interdum, justo lectus sagittis dui, et vehicula libero dui cursus dui. Mauris tempor ligula sed lacus. Duis cursus enim ut augue. Cras ac magna. Cras nulla. Nulla egestas. Curabitur a leo. Quisque egestas wisi eget nunc. Nam feugiat lacus vel est. Curabitur consectetuer.

Suspendisse vel felis. Ut lorem lorem, interdum eu, tincidunt sit amet, laoreet vitae, arcu. Aenean faucibus pede eu ante. Praesent enim elit, rutrum at, molestie non, nonummy vel, nisl. Ut lectus eros, malesuada sit amet, fermentum eu, sodales cursus, magna. Donec eu purus. Quisque vehicula, urna sed ultricies auctor, pede lorem egestas dui, et convallis elit erat sed nulla. Donec luctus. Curabitur et nunc. Aliquam dolor odio, commodo pretium, ultricies non, pharetra in, velit. Integer arcu est, nonummy in, fermentum faucibus, egestas vel, odio.

Sed commodo posuere pede. Mauris ut est. Ut quis purus. Sed ac odio. Sed vehicula hendrerit sem. Duis non odio. Morbi ut dui. Sed accumsan risus eget odio. In hac habitasse platea dictumst. Pellentesque non elit. Fusce sed justo eu urna porta tincidunt. Mauris felis odio, sollicitudin sed, volutpat a, ornare ac, erat. Morbi quis dolor. Donec pellentesque, erat ac sagittis semper, nunc dui lobortis purus, quis congue purus metus ultricies tellus. Proin et quam. Class aptent taciti sociosqu ad litora torquent per conubia nostra, per inceptos hymenaeos. Praesent sapien turpis, fermentum vel, eleifend faucibus, vehicula eu, lacus.

Pellentesque habitant morbi tristique senectus et netus et malesuada fames ac turpis egestas. Donec odio elit, dictum in, hendrerit sit amet, egestas sed, leo. Praesent feugiat sapien aliquet odio. Integer vitae justo. Aliquam vestibulum fringilla lorem. Sed neque lectus, consectetuer at, consectetuer sed, eleifend ac, lectus. Nulla facilisi. Pellentesque eget lectus. Proin eu metus. Sed porttitor. In hac habitasse platea dictumst. Suspendisse eu lectus. Ut mi mi, lacinia sit amet, placerat et, mollis vitae, dui. Sed ante tellus, tristique ut, iaculis eu, malesuada ac, dui. Mauris nibh leo, facilisis non, adipiscing quis, ultricies a, dui.

Morbi luctus, wisi viverra faucibus pretium, nibh est placerat odio, nec commodo wisi enim eget quam. Quisque libero justo, consectetuer a, feugiat vitae, porttitor eu, libero. Suspendisse sed mauris vitae elit sollicitudin malesuada. Maecenas ultricies eros sit amet ante. Ut venenatis velit. Maecenas

---

Lorem ipsum dolor sit amet, consectetuer adipiscing elit. Ut purus elit, vestibulum ut, placerat ac, adipiscing vitae, felis. Curabitur dictum gravida mauris. Nam arcu libero, nonummy eget, consectetuer id, vulputate a, magna. Donec vehicula augue eu neque. Pellentesque habitant morbi tristique senectus et netus et malesuada fames ac turpis egestas. Mauris ut leo. Cras viverra metus rhoncus sem. Nulla et lectus vestibulum urna fringilla ultrices. Phasellus eu tellus sit amet tortor gravida placerat. Integer sapien est, iaculis in, pretium quis, viverra ac, nunc. Praesent eget sem vel leo ultrices bibendum. Aenean faucibus. Morbi dolor nulla, malesuada eu, pulvinar at, mollis ac, nulla. Curabitur auctor semper nulla. Donec varius orci eget risus. Duis nibh mi, congue eu, accumsan eleifend, sagittis quis, diam. Duis eget orci sit amet orci dignissim rutrum.

Nam dui ligula, fringilla a, euismod sodales, sollicitudin vel, wisi. Morbi auctor lorem non justo. Nam lacus libero, pretium at, lobortis vitae, ultricies et, tellus. Donec aliquet, tortor sed accumsan bibendum, erat ligula aliquet magna, vitae ornare odio metus a mi. Morbi ac orci et nisl hendrerit mollis. Suspendisse ut massa. Cras nec ante. Pellentesque a nulla. Cum sociis natoque penatibus et magnis dis parturient montes, nascetur ridiculus mus. Aliquam tincidunt urna. Nulla ullamcorper vestibulum turpis. Pellentesque cursus luctus mauris.

Nulla malesuada porttitor diam. Donec felis erat, congue non, volutpat at, tincidunt tristique, libero. Vivamus viverra fermentum felis. Donec nonummy pellentesque ante. Phasellus adipiscing semper elit. Proin fermentum massa ac quam. Sed diam turpis, molestie vitae, placerat a, molestie nec, leo. Maecenas lacinia. Nam ipsum ligula, eleifend at, accumsan nec, suscipit a, ipsum. Morbi blandit ligula feugiat magna. Nunc eleifend consequat lorem. Sed lacinia nulla vitae enim. Pellentesque tincidunt purus vel magna. Integer non enim. Praesent euismod nunc eu purus. Donec bibendum quam in tellus. Nullam cursus pulvinar lectus. Donec et mi. Nam vulputate metus eu enim. Vestibulum pellentesque felis eu massa.

Quisque ullamcorper placerat ipsum. Cras nibh. Morbi vel justo vitae lacus tincidunt ultrices. Lorem ipsum dolor sit amet, consectetuer adipiscing elit. In hac habitasse platea dictumst. Integer tempus convallis augue. Etiam facilisis. Nunc elementum fermentum wisi. Aenean placerat. Ut imperdiet, enim sed gravida sollicitudin, felis odio placerat quam, ac pulvinar elit purus eget enim. Nunc vitae tortor. Proin tempus nibh sit amet nisl. Vivamus

---

at, tincidunt tristique, libero. Vivamus viverra fermentum felis. Donec nonummy pellentesque ante. Phasellus adipiscing semper elit. Proin fermentum massa ac quam. Sed diam turpis, molestie vitae, placerat a, molestie nec, leo. Maecenas lacinia. Nam ipsum ligula, eleifend at, accumsan nec, suscipit a, ipsum. Morbi blandit ligula feugiat magna. Nunc eleifend consequat lorem. Sed lacinia nulla vitae enim. Pellentesque tincidunt purus vel magna. Integer non enim. Praesent euismod nunc eu purus. Donec bibendum quam in tellus. Nullam cursus pulvinar lectus. Donec et mi. Nam vulputate metus eu enim. Vestibulum pellentesque felis eu massa.

Quisque ullamcorper placerat ipsum. Cras nibh. Morbi vel justo vitae lacus tincidunt ultrices. Lorem ipsum dolor sit amet, consectetuer adipiscing elit. In hac habitasse platea dictumst. Integer tempus convallis augue. Etiam facilisis. Nunc elementum fermentum wisi. Aenean placerat. Ut imperdiet, enim sed gravida sollicitudin, felis odio placerat quam, ac pulvinar elit purus eget enim. Nunc vitae tortor. Proin tempus nibh sit amet nisl. Vivamus quis tortor vitae risus porta vehicula.

Fusce mauris. Vestibulum luctus nibh at lectus. Sed bibendum, nulla a faucibus semper, leo velit ultricies tellus, ac venenatis arcu wisi vel nisl. Vestibulum diam. Aliquam pellentesque, augue quis sagittis posuere, turpis lacus congue quam, in hendrerit risus eros eget felis. Maecenas eget erat in sapien mattis porttitor. Vestibulum porttitor. Nulla facilisi. Sed a turpis eu lacus commodo facilisis. Morbi fringilla, wisi in dignissim interdum, justo lectus sagittis dui, et vehicula libero dui cursus dui. Mauris tempor ligula sed lacus. Duis cursus enim ut augue. Cras ac magna. Cras nulla. Nulla egestas. Curabitur a leo. Quisque egestas wisi eget nunc. Nam feugiat lacus vel est. Curabitur consectetuer.

Suspendisse vel felis. Ut lorem lorem, interdum eu, tincidunt sit amet, laoreet vitae, arcu. Aenean faucibus pede eu ante. Praesent enim elit, rutrum at, molestie non, nonummy vel, nisl. Ut lectus eros, malesuada sit amet, fermentum eu, sodales cursus, magna. Donec eu purus. Quisque vehicula, urna sed ultricies auctor, pede lorem egestas dui, et convallis elit erat sed nulla. Donec luctus. Curabitur et nunc. Aliquam dolor odio, commodo pretium, ultricies non, pharetra in, velit. Integer arcu est, nonummy in, fermentum faucibus, egestas vel, odio.

Sed commodo posuere pede. Mauris ut est. Ut quis purus. Sed ac odio. Sed vehicula hendrerit sem. Duis non odio. Morbi ut dui. Sed accumsan risus eget odio. In hac habitasse platea dictumst. Pellentesque non elit. Fusce sed justo eu urna porta tincidunt. Mauris felis odio, sollicitudin sed, volutpat a, ornare ac, erat. Morbi quis dolor. Donec pellentesque, erat ac sagittis semper, nunc dui lobortis purus, quis congue purus metus ultricies tellus. Proin et quam. Class aptent taciti sociosqu ad litora torquent per

---

Etiam ac leo a risus tristique nonummy. Donec dignissim tincidunt nulla. Vestibulum rhoncus molestie odio. Sed lobortis, justo et pretium lobortis, mauris turpis condimentum augue, nec ultricies nibh arcu pretium enim. Nunc purus neque, placerat id, imperdiet sed, pellentesque nec, nisl. Vestibulum imperdiet neque non sem accumsan laoreet. In hac habitasse platea dictumst. Etiam condimentum facilisis libero. Aliquam porttitor nisl nec aliquam dapibus. Pellentesque auctor sapien. Sed egestas sapien nec lectus. Pellentesque vel dui vel neque bibendum viverra. Aliquam porttitor nisl nec pede. Proin mattis libero vel turpis. Donec rutrum mauris et libero. Proin euismod porta felis. Nam lobortis, metus quis elementum condimentum, nunc lectus elementum mauris, eget vulputate ligula tellus eu neque. Vivamus eu dolor.

Lorem ipsum dolor sit amet, consectetuer adipiscing elit. Ut purus elit, vestibulum ut, placerat ac, adipiscing vitae, felis. Curabitur dictum gravida mauris. Nam arcu libero, nonummy eget, consectetuer id, vulputate a, magna. Donec vehicula augue eu neque. Pellentesque habitant morbi tristique senectus et netus et malesuada fames ac turpis egestas. Mauris ut leo. Cras viverra metus rhoncus sem. Nulla et lectus vestibulum urna fringilla ultrices. Phasellus eu tellus sit amet tortor gravida placerat. Integer sapien est, iaculis in, pretium quis, viverra ac, nunc. Praesent eget sem vel leo ultrices bibendum. Aenean faucibus. Morbi dolor nulla, malesuada eu, pulvinar at, mollis ac, nulla. Curabitur auctor semper nulla. Donec varius orci eget risus. Duis nibh mi, congue eu, accumsan eleifend, sagittis quis, diam. Duis eget orci sit amet orci dignissim rutrum.

Nam dui ligula, fringilla a, euismod sodales, sollicitudin vel, wisi. Morbi auctor lorem non justo. Nam lacus libero, pretium at, lobortis vitae, ultricies et, tellus. Donec aliquet, tortor sed accumsan bibendum, erat ligula aliquet magna, vitae ornare odio metus a mi. Morbi ac orci et nisl hendrerit mollis. Suspendisse ut massa. Cras nec ante. Pellentesque a nulla. Cum sociis natoque penatibus et magnis dis parturient montes, nascetur ridiculus mus. Aliquam tincidunt urna. Nulla ullamcorper vestibulum turpis. Pellentesque cursus luctus mauris.

Nulla malesuada porttitor diam. Donec felis erat, congue non, volutpat

---

at, tincidunt tristique, libero. Vivamus viverra fermentum felis. Donec nonummy pellentesque ante. Phasellus adipiscing semper elit. Proin fermentum massa ac quam. Sed diam turpis, molestie vitae, placerat a, molestie nec, leo. Maecenas lacinia. Nam ipsum ligula, eleifend at, accumsan nec, suscipit a, ipsum. Morbi blandit ligula feugiat magna. Nunc eleifend consequat lorem. Sed lacinia nulla vitae enim. Pellentesque tincidunt purus vel magna. Integer non enim. Praesent euismod nunc eu purus. Donec bibendum quam in tellus. Nullam cursus pulvinar lectus. Donec et mi. Nam vulputate metus eu enim. Vestibulum pellentesque felis eu massa.

Quisque ullamcorper placerat ipsum. Cras nibh. Morbi vel justo vitae lacus tincidunt ultrices. Lorem ipsum dolor sit amet, consectetuer adipiscing elit. In hac habitasse platea dictumst. Integer tempus convallis augue. Etiam facilisis. Nunc elementum fermentum wisi. Aenean placerat. Ut imperdiet, enim sed gravida sollicitudin, felis odio placerat quam, ac pulvinar elit purus eget enim. Nunc vitae tortor. Proin tempus nibh sit amet nisl. Vivamus quis tortor vitae risus porta vehicula.

Fusce mauris. Vestibulum luctus nibh at lectus. Sed bibendum, nulla a faucibus semper, leo velit ultricies tellus, ac venenatis arcu wisi vel nisl. Vestibulum diam. Aliquam pellentesque, augue quis sagittis posuere, turpis lacus congue quam, in hendrerit risus eros eget felis. Maecenas eget erat in sapien mattis porttitor. Vestibulum porttitor. Nulla facilisi. Sed a turpis eu lacus commodo facilisis. Morbi fringilla, wisi in dignissim interdum, justo lectus sagittis dui, et vehicula libero dui cursus dui. Mauris tempor ligula sed lacus. Duis cursus enim ut augue. Cras ac magna. Cras nulla. Nulla egestas. Curabitur a leo. Quisque egestas wisi eget nunc. Nam feugiat lacus vel est. Curabitur consectetuer.

Suspendisse vel felis. Ut lorem lorem, interdum eu, tincidunt sit amet, laoreet vitae, arcu. Aenean faucibus pede eu ante. Praesent enim elit, rutrum at, molestie non, nonummy vel, nisl. Ut lectus eros, malesuada sit amet, fermentum eu, sodales cursus, magna. Donec eu purus. Quisque vehicula, urna sed ultricies auctor, pede lorem egestas dui, et convallis elit erat sed nulla. Donec luctus. Curabitur et nunc. Aliquam dolor odio, commodo pretium, ultricies non, pharetra in, velit. Integer arcu est, nonummy in, fermentum faucibus, egestas vel, odio.

Sed commodo posuere pede. Mauris ut est. Ut quis purus. Sed ac odio. Sed vehicula hendrerit sem. Duis non odio. Morbi ut dui. Sed accumsan risus eget odio. In hac habitasse platea dictumst. Pellentesque non elit. Fusce sed justo eu urna porta tincidunt. Mauris felis odio, sollicitudin sed, volutpat a, ornare ac, erat. Morbi quis dolor. Donec pellentesque, erat ac sagittis semper, nunc dui lobortis purus, quis congue purus metus ultricies tellus. Proin et quam. Class aptent taciti sociosqu ad litora torquent per

A widow (top) and orphan (bottom).

acters in a line, hoping to make the line fit without the need for hyphenation. Of course, if taken to extremes, this would remove all hyphens, but make the page unreadable! Shrinking or stretching by up to 2% seems to be hard to notice, though. Can you spot the use of microtypography in the paragraphs of this book?

Another way to improve the look of a paragraph is to allow punctuation to hang over the end of the line. For example, a comma or a hyphen should hang a little over the right hand side – this makes the block of the paragraph seem visually more straight, even though really we have made it less straight. Here is a narrow paragraph without overhanging punctuation (left), then with (middle):

One morning, when Gregor Samsa woke from troubled dreams, he found himself trans-formed in his bed into a horrible vermin. He lay on his armour-like back, and if he lifted his head a little he could see his brown belly, slightly domed and divided...	One morning, when Gregor Samsa woke from troubled dreams, he found himself trans-formed in his bed into a horrible vermin. He lay on his armour-like back, and if he lifted his head a little he could see his brown belly, slightly domed and divided...	One morning, when Gregor Samsa woke from troubled dreams, he found himself trans-formed in his bed into a horrible vermin. He lay on his armour-like back, and if he lifted his head a little he could see his brown belly, slightly domed and divided...

The vertical line (far right) highlights the overhanging hyphens and commas used to keep the right hand margin visually straight. A further distracting visual problem in paragraphs is that of *rivers*. These are the vertical lines of white space which occur when spaces on successive lines are in just the wrong place:

interdum sem, dapibus sempe
et augue. Quisque cursus nul
ıauris malesuada mollis. Nulla
; arcu, egestas ac, fermentum c
s, sem in pretium fermentum,
;equat augue urna in wisi. Qui
ıuis, lacinia in, est. Fusce facilis

interdum sem, dapibus sempe
et augue. Quisque cursus nul
ıauris malesuada mollis. Nullɛ
; arcu, egestas ac, fermentum c
s, sem in pretium fermentum,
;equat augue urna in wisi. Quɩ
ɩuis, lacinia in, est. Fusce facilis

We have shown the river with a line. Notice that the word "fermentum" appearing in almost the same place on two successive lines is also distracting. The problem is difficult to deal with automatically, and the text may have to be edited to fix it. The microtypographical techniques discussed above can help a little – since there are fewer widened spaces between words, the rivers will be narrower and less noticeable.

You may wonder how type was set before computers. In much the same way, it turns out, but with many more manual steps and a lot of little pieces of metal. Here is one such piece, for the character "n" at a particular size, in a particular typeface:

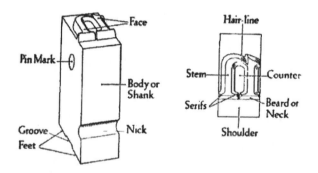

These are picked from a tray of boxes, by hand, and placed into rows into a *composing stick*, each word separated by little metal spaces, each row spaced by a metal strip (the leading). You can imagine that many many copies of these little metal pieces were required for each typeface and size, so it was an expensive business. Because it will eventually be used for printing by being inked and stamped or rolled on paper, the type is mirrored, and hard to read, and one must be careful not to mix up "p" and "q", or "b" and "d". (This is one possible origin of the phrase "mind your Ps and Qs".) This painstaking process is shown on the opposite page.

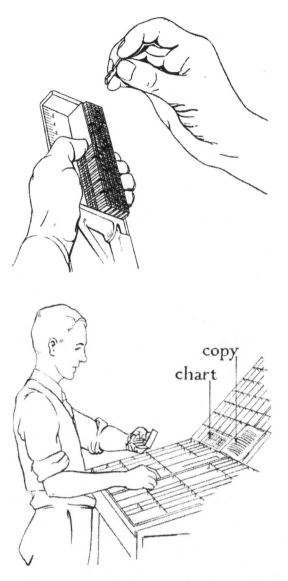

copy
chart

The finished paragraphs of type are arranged in a *galley*. This will be used to make prints of the page (or pages – two or four may be printed from one galley, then folded and cut). You can imagine how long it takes to make up the galleys for a book, and how much time is required to justify each line by inserting exactly the right spaces and hyphenating by hand. Mistakes found after test prints can be very costly to fix, since they necessitate taking apart the

galley and replacing not just a single character, but perhaps re-
typesetting a whole paragraph. Here is a galley, ready for printing:

Eventually, machines were developed to automatically place
the pieces of type based on what was typed on a keyboard and to
automatically justify each line. Such mechanical systems were in
common use until the advent of so-called phototypesetting. This
involved building an image by shining light through a series of sten-
cils onto photosensitive paper, then photographing it. Computer
typesetting supplanted both in the late twentieth century.

Problems

Solutions on page 166.

Identify good hyphenation points in the following words:

1. hyphenation

2. fundraising

3. arithmetic (noun)

4. arithmetic (adjective)

5. demonstration

6. demonstrative

7. genuine

8. mountainous

Solutions

Chapter 1

1

For the diamond, if we start on the left hand side, we have (2,10)—(10,18)—(18,10)—(10,2)—(2,10). For the star, if we start at the bottom left point, we have (3,3)—(10,19)—(17,3)—(1,13)—(19,13)—(3,3).

2

We see a crude representation of the letter E, and the Maltese cross.

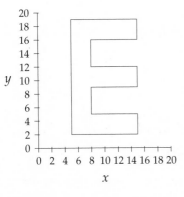 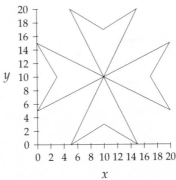

3

For example:

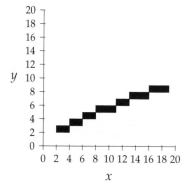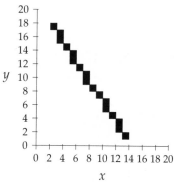

4

For example:

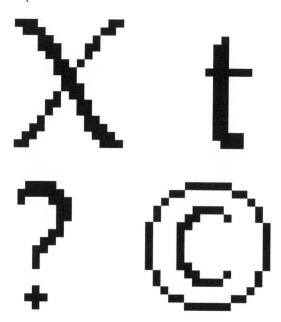

Chapter 2

1

We assign the letters ABCD as in the chapter text:

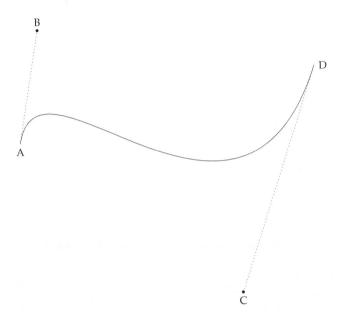

Now, we continue the construction as before, making sure we are not confused by the fact that the line BC now crosses the curve:

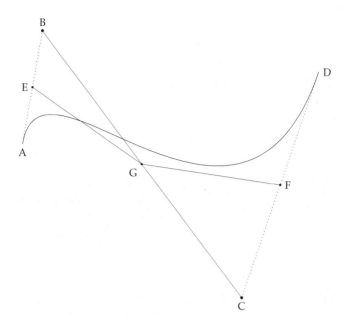

Finally, we finish the construction all the way to J, so our diagram looks like this:

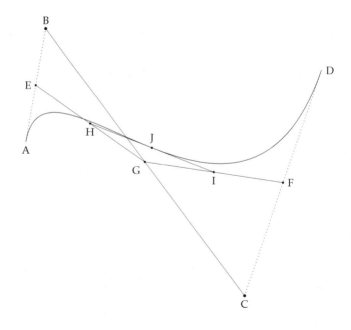

So we have the new Bézier curves AEHJ and JIFD as before:

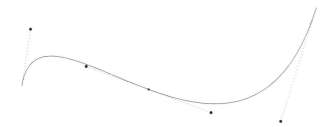

3

With the even-odd rule:

With the non-zero rule:

Chapter 3

1

32-11-42-54-23-11-14-11-31-24-44-44-31-15-31-11-32-12. There are 18 characters in the message, and so 36 numbers to transmit (though in Polybius's system of torches, these would be done two at a time, so just 18 distinct actions). We might use Z for the space character, since it doesn't appear often in normal text. We could use ZZZ for end of message.

2

We have 32 rows:

Bits	Number	Letter	Bits	Number	Letter
00000	0	A	10000	16	Q
00001	1	B	10001	17	R
00010	2	C	10010	18	S
00011	3	D	10011	19	T
00100	4	E	10100	20	U
00101	5	F	10101	21	V
00110	6	G	10110	22	W
00111	7	H	10111	23	X
01000	8	I	11000	24	Y
01001	9	J	11001	25	Z
01010	10	K	11010	26	*space*
01011	11	L	11011	27	.
01100	12	M	11100	28	,
01101	13	N	11101	29	:
01110	14	O	11110	30	;
01111	15	P	11111	31	?

Here, we choose the capital letters and the punctuation *space . , : ; ?* and hope this covers most useful messages.

3

Treason is very much a matter of habit, Smiley decided.

4

84 104 101 109 111 114 101 105 100 101 110 116 105 116 105 101 115
97 109 97 110 104 97 115 44 116 104 101 109 111 114 101 116 104 101
121 101 120 112 114 101 115 115 116 104 101 112 101 114 115 111 110
116 104 101 121 99 111 110 99 101 97 108 46

5

a) The love of money is the root of *all* evil.

b) The love of \$\$\$ is the root of all evil.

c) The love of $\$\$\$\$$ is the root of all evil.

d) The love of *\$$\$$\$* is the root of all evil.

Chapter 4

1

a) The pattern does not match.

b) The pattern matches at position 17.

c) The pattern matches at positions 28 and 35.

d) The pattern matches at position 24.

2

a) The texts aa, aaa, and aaa etc. match.

b) The texts ac and abc only match.

c) The texts ac, abc, and abbc etc. match.

d) The texts ad, abd, acd, abbd, accd, abcd, acbd, and abbbd etc. match.

3

a) The pattern matches at positions 16 and 17.

b) The pattern matches at positions 0 and 24.

c) The pattern matches at positions 0, 1, 24, and 25.

d) The pattern matches at postiions 0, 1, 24, and 25.

Chapter 6

1

Letter	Frequency	Code	Letter	Frequency	Code
space	41	111	u	5	110100
e	18	100	v	4	110011
o	14	1011	w	4	110010
t	14	0111	f	4	110001
a	13	0110	'	4	010111
h	12	0100	y	3	010101
r	11	0011	.	3	01010000
n	11	0010	,	3	01010001
s	10	0000	p	2	01010010
i	9	11011	I	2	01010011
c	8	10101	q	1	01011000
m	6	10100	E	1	01011001
l	6	00011	S	1	01011010
g	6	110101	T	1	01011011

So we have:

```
'        I               h    a    v      e         a
010111 01010011 111 0100 0110 110011 100 111 0110 111
t    h    e    o    r    y         w      h    i
0111 0100 100 1011 0011 010101 111 110010 0100 11011
c     h         I           s    u       s      p
10101 0100 111 01010011 111 0000 110100 0000 01010010
e    c     t         i    s        r    a    t    h
100 10101 0111 111 11011 0000 111 0011 0110 0111 0100
e    r          i    m     m     o    r    a    l
100 0011 111 11011 10100 10100 1011 0011 0110 00011
,          '         S    m     i     l    e      y
01010001 010111 111 01011010 10100 11011 00011 100 010101
     w      e    n    t       o    n     ,
111 110010 100 0010 0111 111 1011 0010 01010001 111
m     o    r    e         l     i    g      h    t
10100 1011 0011 100 111 00011 11011 110101 0100 0111
l      y          .
00011 010101 01010000
```

2

There are moments which are made up of too much stuff for them to be lived at the time they occur.

3

The lengths and colours are:

Colour	Length	Code	Colour	Length	Code
White	37	00010110	White	10	00111
White	5	1100	White	2	0111
Black	2	11	Black	8	000101
White	7	1111	White	3	1000
Black	7	00011	Black	2	11
White	7	1111	White	5	1100
Black	6	0010	Black	3	10
White	3	1000	White	2	0111
White	4	1011	Black	2	11
Black	4	011	White	10	00111
White	5	1100	White	2	0111
Black	9	000100	Black	8	000101
White	4	1011	White	3	1000
Black	9	000100	Black	2	11
White	2	0111	White	6	1110
White	4	1011	Black	2	11
Black	4	011	White	2	0111
White	5	1100	Black	2	11
Black	2	11	White	7	1111
White	5	1100	Black	2	11
Black	3	10	White	1	0000111
White	3	1000	White	1	0000111
Black	2	11	Black	3	10
White	5	1100	White	4	1011
Black	3	10	Black	3	10
White	1	0000111	White	2	0111
White	4	1011	Black	2	11

Black	5	0011	White	6	1110
White	4	1011	Black	2	11
Black	2	11	White	2	0111
White	6	1110	Black	3	10
Black	2	11	White	6	1110
White	2	0111	Black	2	11
Black	2	11	White	1	0000111
White	7	1111	White	1	0000111
Black	2	11	Black	2	11
White	1	0000111	White	6	1110
White	3	1000	Black	2	11
Black	2	11	White	2	0111
White	2	0111	Black	2	11
Black	2	11	White	6	1110
White	4	1011	Black	2	11
Black	2	11	White	3	1000
White	5	1100	Black	2	11
Black	3	10	White	5	1100
White	2	0111	Black	3	10
Black	2	11	White	1	0000111
White	10	00111	White	1	0000111
White	3	1000	Black	2	11
Black	2	11	White	6	1110
White	2	0111	Black	3	10
Black	2	11	White	1	0000111
White	4	1011	Black	10	0000100
Black	9	000100	White	3	1000
White	3	1000	Black	9	000100
Black	2	11	White	2	0111
White	10	00111	Black	2	11
White	2	0111	White	8	1011
Black	3	10	Black	2	11
White	2	0111	White	2	0111
Black	3	10	Black	7	00011
White	3	1000	White	6	1110

Black	9	000100	Black	7	00011
White	3	1000	White	3	1000
Black	2	11	White	37	00010110

So we have:

```
0001011011001111110001111110010100010110111100000010
0101100010001111011011110011110010100011110011000001
1110110011101111110110111111111110000111100011011 1
0101011111100100111110011110001101111110110001001 00
0110011101111001110100000010010001100111011100010 1
1000111110110111111111110000111000011110101110101 11
1111011100011111011000011100001111111101101011111 110
1110001111001000001110000111111111010000011100001011
0000001000111111011110111000111110000101100000010 11
0
```

4

The codes are:

Code	Length	Colour	Code	Length	Colour
00010110	37	White	000100	9	Black
0000111	1	White	0111	2	White
00011	7	Black	11	2	Black
1111	7	White	1100	5	White
00011	7	Black	10	3	Black
1100	5	White	0111	2	White
00011	7	Black	11	2	Black
1000	3	White	1011	8	White
000100	9	Black	11	2	Black
1011	4	White	0111	2	White
0000100	10	Black	11	2	Black
1000	3	White	1100	5	White
000100	9	Black	10	3	Black
0111	2	White	0000111	1	White
11	2	Black	11	2	Black
1100	5	White	1110	6	White
10	3	Black	11	2	Black

1000	3	White	0111	2	White
10	3	Black	11	2	Black
1100	5	White	1011	8	White
10	3	Black	11	2	Black
0111	2	White	0111	2	White
11	2	Black	11	2	Black
1100	5	White	1110	6	White
10	3	Black	11	2	Black
0000111	1	White	0000111	1	White
11	2	Black	11	2	Black
1110	6	White	1110	6	White
11	2	Black	11	2	Black
0111	2	White	0111	2	White
10	3	Black	10	3	Black
1111	7	White	1110	6	White
11	2	Black	10	3	Black
0111	2	White	0111	2	White
11	2	Black	11	2	Black
1110	6	White	1110	6	White
11	2	Black	11	2	Black
0000111	1	White	0000111	1	White
11	2	Black	11	2	Black
1100	5	White	1110	6	White
10	3	Black	11	2	Black
0111	2	White	0111	2	White
11	2	Black	011	4	Black
1011	8	White	1100	5	White
11	2	Black	11	2	Black
0111	2	White	1000	3	White
11	2	Black	11	2	Black
1100	5	White	1110	6	White
10	3	Black	11	2	Black
0000111	1	White	0000111	1	White
000100	9	Black	0000100	10	Black
1000	3	White	1000	3	White

11	2	Black	0000100	10	Black
1011	8	White	1000	3	White
11	2	Black	000100	9	Black
0111	2	White	0111	2	White
000100	9	Black	0000111	1	White
0111	2	White	00011	7	Black
000100	9	Black	1111	7	White
1000	3	White	0010	6	Black
11	2	Black	1110	6	White
1011	8	White	0010	6	Black
11	2	Black	1011	4	White
0111	2	White	00010110	37	White

So we have the image:

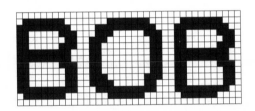

Chapter 7

1

a)

$$\frac{(1+1)+1}{2+1} \implies$$
$$\implies 3$$

b)

$$(2 \times 2) \times 2$$
$$\implies \quad \underline{4 \times 2}$$
$$\implies \quad 8$$

c)

$$(2 \times 3) + 4$$
$$\implies \quad \underline{6 + 4}$$
$$\implies \quad 10$$

2

a)

$$x \times x \times y$$
$$\implies \quad \underline{4 \times 4} \times 5$$
$$\implies \quad \underline{16 \times 5}$$
$$\implies \quad 80$$

$$z \times y + z$$
$$\implies \quad \underline{100 \times 5} + 100$$
$$\implies \quad \underline{500 + 100}$$
$$\implies \quad 600$$

b)

$$z \times z$$
$$\implies \quad \underline{100 \times 100}$$
$$\implies \quad 10000$$

3

a)

$$f\ 4\ 5$$
$$\implies\quad 4 \times 5 \times 4$$
$$\implies\quad 20 \times 4$$
$$\implies\quad 80$$

b)

$$f\ (f\ 4\ 5)\ 5$$
$$\implies\quad f\ 80\ 5$$
$$\implies\quad 80 \times 5 \times 80$$
$$\implies\quad 400 \times 80$$
$$\implies\quad 32000$$

c)

$$f\ (f\ 4\ 5)\ (f\ 4\ 5)$$
$$\implies\quad f\ 80\ 80$$
$$\implies\quad 80 \times 80\ \times 80$$
$$\implies\quad 32000 \times 80$$
$$\implies\quad 512000$$

4

a)

$$f\ 5\ 4 = f\ 4\ 5$$
$$\implies\quad 80 = 80$$
$$\implies\quad \text{true}$$

b)

$$\text{if } 1 = 2 \text{ then 3 else 4}$$
$$\implies\quad \text{if false then 3 else 4}$$
$$\implies\quad 4$$

c)

$$\frac{\text{if (if } 1 = 2 \text{ then false else true) then 3 else 4}}{}$$
$$\implies \quad \underline{\text{if true then 3 else 4}}$$
$$\implies \quad 3$$

5

a)

$$\frac{\text{head } [2,3,4]}{}$$
$$\implies \quad 2$$

b)

$$\frac{\text{tail } [2]}{}$$
$$\implies \quad []$$

c)

$$\frac{\text{head } [2,3,4] \bullet [2,3,4]}{}$$
$$\implies \quad \underline{[2] \bullet [2,3,4]}$$
$$\implies \quad [2,2,3,4]$$

6

a) $[]$ (first if)

b) $[1]$ (second if)

c) $[1,3]$ (via $1 \bullet \text{odds } []$)

Chapter 8

1

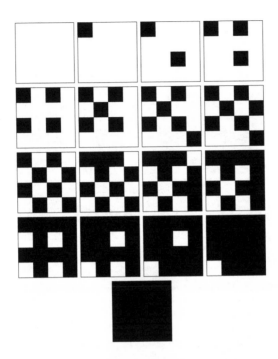

2

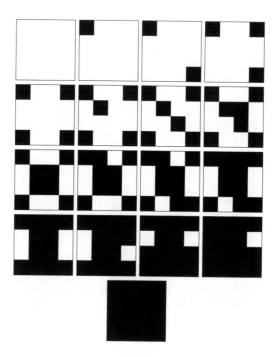

3

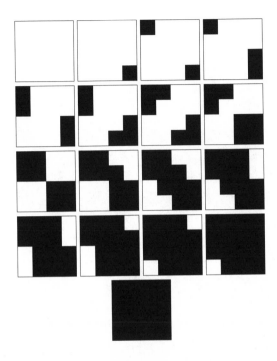

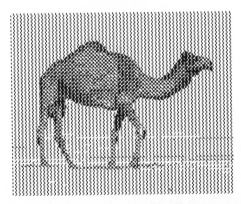

Chapter 9

1

Palatino

2

AVERSION

3

Conjecture

Chapter 10

1

hy-phen-a-tion

2

fund-raising

3

re-cord (the verb)

4

rec-ord (the noun)

5

a-rith-me-tic (the noun)

6

ar-ith-me-tic (the adjective)

7

dem-on-stra-tion

8

de-mon-stra-tive

9

gen-u-ine

10

moun-tain-ous

Further Reading

There follows a list of interesting books for each chapter. Some are closely related to the chapter contents, some tangentially. The level of expertise required to understand each of them varies quite a bit, but do not be afraid to read books you do not understand all of, especially if you can obtain or borrow them at little cost.

Chapter 1

Computer Graphics: Principles and Practice James D. Foley, Andries van Dam, Steven K. Fiener, and John F. Hughes. Published by Addison Wesley (second edition, 1995). ISBN 0201848406.

Contemporary Newspaper Design: Shaping the News in the Digital Age – Typography & Image on Modern Newsprint John D. Berry and Roger Black. Published by Mark Batty (2007). ISBN 0972424032.

Chapter 2

A Book of Curves E. H. Lockwood. Published by Cambridge University Press (1961). ISBN 0521044448.

Fifty Typefaces That Changed the World: Design Museum Fifty John L. Waters. Published by Conran (2013). ISBN 184091629X.

Thinking with Type: A Critical Guide for Designers, Writers, Editors, and Students Ellen Lupton. Published by Princeton Architectural Press (second edition, 2010). ISBN 1568989695.

Chapter 3

The Histories Polybius (translated by Robin Waterfield). Published by Oxford University Press under the Oxford World Classics imprint (2010). ISBN 0199534705.

Code: The Hidden Language of Computer Hardware and Software Charles Petzold. Published by Microsoft Press (2000). ISBN 0735611319.

Unicode Explained Jukka K. Korpela. Published by O'Reilly Media (2006). ISBN 059610121X.

The Decipherment of Linear B John Chadwick. Published by Cambridge University Press (second edition, 1967). ISBN 1107691761.

Chapter 4

Introduction to Algorithms T. Cormen, C. Leiserson, R. Rivest, and C. Stein. Published by MIT Press (third edition, 2009). ISBN 0262533057.

Flexible Pattern Matching in Strings: Practical On-Line Search Algorithms for Texts and Biological Sequences Gonzalo Navarro and Mathieu Raffinot. Published by Cambridge University Press (2007). ISBN 0521039932.

Google's PageRank and Beyond: The Science of Search Engine Rankings Amy N. Langville and Carl D. Meyer. Published by Princeton University Press (2012). ISBN 0691152667.

Chapter 5

The Wonderful Writing Machine Bruce Bliven, Jr. Published by Random House (1954). ISBN 600150329X.

Quirky Qwerty: The Story of the Keyboard @ Your Fingertips Torbjörn Lundmark. Published by University of New South Wales Press (2001). ISBN 0868404365.

The Iron Whim : A Fragmented History of Typewriting Darren Wershler-Henry. Published by McClelland & Stewart (2005). ISBN 0771089252.

Chapter 6

Fundamental Data Compression Ida Mengyi Pu. Published by Butterworth-Heinemann (2006). ISBN 0750663103.

The Fax Modem Sourcebook Andrew Margolis. Published by Wiley (1995). ISBN 0471950726.

Introduction to Data Compression Khalid Sayood. Published by Morgan Kaufman in The Morgan Kaufmann Series in Multimedia Information and Systems (fourth edition, 2012). ISBN 0124157963.

Chapter 7

Python Programming for the Absolute Beginner Mike Dawson. Published by Course Technology PTR (third edition, 2010). ISBN 1435455002.

OCaml from the Very Beginning John Whitington. Published by Coherent Press (2013). ISBN 0957671105.

Seven Languages in Seven Weeks: A Pragmatic Guide to Learning Programming Languages Bruce A. Tate. Published by Pragmatic Bookshelf (2010). ISBN 193435659X.

Chapter 8

How to Identify Prints Bamber Gascgoine. Published by Thames & Hudson (second edition, 2004). ISBN 0500284806.

A History of Engraving and Etching Arthur M. Hind. Published by Dover Publications (1963). ISBN 0486209547.

Prints and Printmaking: An Introduction to the History and Techniques Antony Griffiths. Published by University of California Press (1996). ISBN 0520207149.

Digital Halftoning Robert Ulichney. Published by The MIT Press (1987). ISBN 0262210096.

Chapter 9

Just My Type: A Book About Fonts Simon Garfield. Published by Profile Books (2011). ISBN 1846683025.

The Geometry of Type: The Anatomy of 100 Essential Typefaces Stephen Coles. Published by Thames and Hudson Ltd (2013). ISBN 0500241422.

The Elements of Typographic Style Robert Bringhurst. Published by Hartley & Marks (2004). ISBN 0881792065.

Chapter 10

Micro-typographic extensions to the T_EX typesetting system PhD Thesis, Hàn Thế Thành, Faculty of Informatics, Masaryk University, Brno, October 2000.

Digital Typography Donald E. Knuth. Published by the Center for the Study of Language and Information (Stanford, California) CSLI Lecture Notes, No. 78 (1999). ISBN 1575860104.

Printer's Type in the Twentieth Century: Manufacturing And Design Methods Richard Southall. Published by Oak Knoll Press (2005). ISBN 1584561552.

History of the Monotype Corporation Judith Slinn et al. Published by Vanbrugh Press (2014). ISBN 0993051005.

Templates

The following pages contain blank templates for answering problems 1.2, 1.3, 1.4, 2.1, 8.1, 8.2, and 8.3.

Problem 1.2

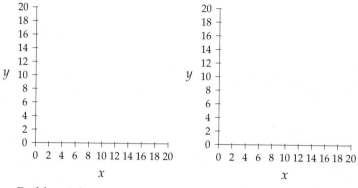

Problem 1.3

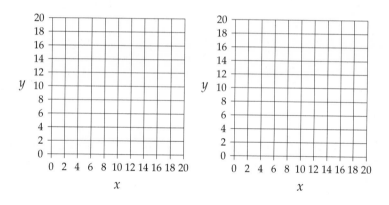

Problem 1.4

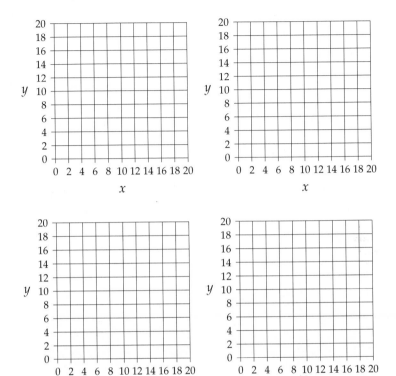

Problem 2.1

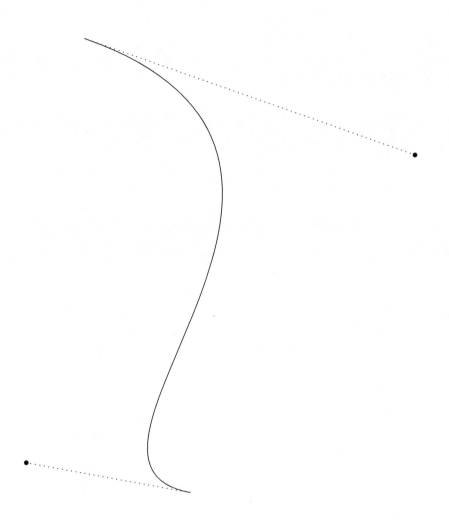

Problem 8.1

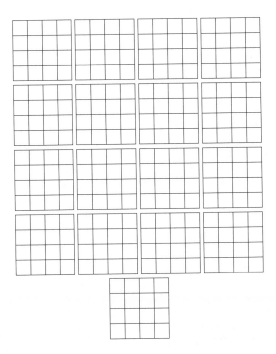

Problem 8.2

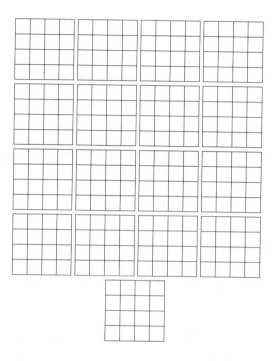

Problem 8.3

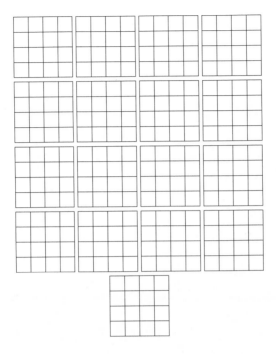

Colophon

This book was designed and typeset by the author using Donald Knuth's TEX system with Leslie Lamport's LATEX macros in 10pt Palatino Linotype, Computer Modern Sans, and Bera Sans Mono. Diagrams were constructed using the tikz package, and the output was prepared by the author as a PDF file for print and eBook formats. In addition, the following packages were used: ragged2e, blindtext, amsmath, etex, gensymb, lettrine, booktabs, placeins, titlesec, makeidx, lineno, nameref, cleveref, xspace, comment, setspace, etoolbox, forest, multicol, tocloft, float, caption, longtable, tabu, enumerate, calc, textcomp, microtype, mathtools, hyperref, fancyhdr, emptypage, underscore, upquote, fancyvrb, idxlayout, xcolor, textgreek. The cover uses typefaces from the Adobe Garamond family.

The eBook was prepared from LATEX sources with latex4ht and Calibre. The physical book was printed by On-Demand Publishing LLC, a subsidiary of Amazon Inc. of Seattle, Washington.

Index

52778810R00124

Made in the USA
Charleston, SC
29 February 2016